CHIPPENHAM

CHIPPENHAM
An East Anglian Estate Village

M. J. Ross

CAEDMON OF WHITBY, Publishers.

ISBN 0 905355 44 X

Published by: CAEDMON OF WHITBY, 128 Upgang Lane,
                 Whitby, North Yorkshire.
Printed by: SMITH SETTLE, Otley, West Yorkshire.

Contents

Preface vi

Introduction vii

Chapter 1: Domesday Book, and the de Mandevilles; 12th century 1

Chapter 2: The Knights Hospitallers; 12th to 15th centuries 5

Chapter 3: The Reformation; 16th century 11

Chapter 4: The Russells, Baronets of Chippenham; 17th century 15

Chapter 5: Admiral Russell, Lord Orford emparks the village 19

Chapter 6: From emparking to enclosure; 18th century 28

Chapter 7: A new dynasty takes over 31

Chapter 8: The estate in Chancery 35

Chapter 9: The English country house 43

Chapter 10: A changing village 51

Chapter 11: The post-war village 55

Chapter 12: The village to-day 59

Appendix 1: The village charities 63

Appendix 2: Listed buildings 68

Family Trees:

    The Russells, Baronets of Chippenham 70

    The Tharps of Chippenham Park, Senior Branch 71

    The Tharps of Chippeham Park, Cadet Branch 72

Preface

Not long after we came to live in the village, Les Drake, the postmaster asked me if I would "bring the village history up to date". I said that I could not do so until I knew more about the village and its residents and that I was, in any case, too busy at the time. The history to which he referred was *An East Anglian Village: or, Epochs in the History of Chippenham (Cambs)* written by the Rev. W. Barber, former vicar of Chippenham, in 1897. It was published privately and is still available in photostat. It is primarily the story of the church rather than the village, and is written in a style very different from my own, so I realised that it could not be "brought up to date" simply by the addition of further "epochs". In preparing this new history, I have, of course, benefitted much from Mr Barber's work.

Dr. Margaret Spufford has written two scholarly works on land use in Chippenham from the earliest times to the eighteenth century in *A Cambridgeshire Community — Chippenham from Settlement to Enclosure* (1965) and *Contrasting Communities* (1974) and I am indebted to her for much that I have written on this aspect of the village. I am grateful to the Very Rev. Hugh Edgell for advice on the Knights Hospitallers (Chap. 2), to David West on the life of Lord Orford (Chap. 5), and to Matthew Slaney for allowing me to see his unpublished Cambridge PhD thesis on the diary of Isaac Archer (1641-1700), Chap. 4). I acknowledge with thanks the permission from Anne Crawley, the present owner of Chippenham Park, to use the extensive Tharp family papers which are in the County Record Office; and I extend those thanks to the County Archivist and his staff and to the curator of the Cambridgeshire Collections in the Central Library.

I have talked to many old residents about changes in the village in their lifetimes, and am particularly grateful to Mary Bowden, Guy and Judy Kent, Ray Simpson, Joyce Smalley and Herbert Watkinson — thank you all, and others not named. For pictures of the village, old and new, I am grateful to Mary Bowden, Anne Crawley, Gordon France, Daphne Hamer, Betty Snare and Derek Coombes, who also took the front cover picture.

I have not included a long list identifying my sources of information and quotations in detail; it would be of no interest to the general reader. My aim has been, simply, to provide residents and visitors with a short up-to-date history of this unusual East Anglian village.

The School House,   *M.J. Ross*
Chippenham   *1995*

vi

Introduction

The village of Chippenham lies four miles north of Newmarket, on the chalk land which runs from N.E. to S.W. across Cambridgeshire, between the Fens to the north and clay lands to the west and south-east. The southern boundary of the parish lies on the main track of the prehistoric Icknield Way, now the B 1506 road from Newmarket to Bury St. Edmunds; the northern boundary includes an inlet of peat fen. The east and west boundaries separate the parish from those of Kennett and Snailwell respectively. The heath land to the south consists of shallow soil over chalk; the fields in the rest of the parish are light well-drained, mainly chalky soil; the fen remains as a small example of original fen vegetation, similar to that of Wicken Fen.

The first sign of the village when approaching Chippenham from the A 11 London to Norwich road is a portion of the great wall, more than three miles long, which surrounds Chippenham Park. Leaving it on the left and passing the north gateway and lodges, the traveller enters the High Street. On the left is "New Row", eight pairs of cottages linked by their washhouses, then the handsome School House opposite the church. At the crossroads at the centre of the village are the village sign, the village pump, two ancient buildings until recently the village shops, and the Tharp Arms public house. Another few hundred yards and the traveller has left the village.

It is not a picture postcard village with thatched houses, a stream and a duck pond, but the traveller can hardly fail to detect that there is something unusual in its character, and many a one stops to inquire and to take photographs. This small village, of some four hundred inhabitants, does indeed have a remarkable history.

Many archaeological traces of early settlements have been found within the parish boundaries, but no reliable written records exist before the most famous date in English history — William the Conqueror, 1066.

Chapter 1

Domesday Book, and the de Mandevilles
12th century

William the Conqueror granted the manor of Chippenham — and other manors in eleven different counties — to Geoffrey de Mandeville, who died in about 1086. This was the year of Domesday Book, the most detailed record of property compiled anywhere during the middle ages. From it we are able to obtain the first reliable evidence of the nature of the village of "Chipeham", as it was therein named. "Manors" did not always share the same boundaries as the "village" settlements of the rural community; a manor might include several villages or a village might be divided between two or more manors, but in Chippenham the manor and the village have always coincided. The hamlet of Badlingham, which lies within the parish of Chippenham, was a separate manor.

In 1086, the area of the manor was about 1000 acres. Its households comprised:-

The Lord of the Manor
19 villeins
13 bordars
6 serfs

a total population of, perhaps, 250.

The lord of the manor's *demesne*, of about 300 acres, was worked by the six slaves, with three ploughs. The villeins cultivated in the open fields in return for specified labour services on the manorial farm; they were neither paid nor did they pay rent. The bordars were cottagers, cultivating much smaller areas of land than the villeins. Under the manorial system, the villagers owed service to the lord of the manor and he was the ultimate source of justice, but they were largely left to organise themselves.

The large open fields were not enclosed. Each farmer worked a certain number of arable strips, which did not lie next to one another; but were spread over the open fields between those of his neighbours. The villeins and bordars had fourteen ploughs between them, and the whole of the land suitable for

1

cultivation was under the plough. One field in three normally lay fallow each year for grazing and manuring. The common pasture for the livestock of the village, which was presumably on the heath land, supported 14 beasts, 3 rounceys (riding horses) and 285 sheep. There was a mill and also a fishery, though this may have been at Wicken Fen rather than Chippenham Fen.

These early villages were self-supporting — and miserably poor — communities. The villagers lived on what they grew and nurtured — vegetables, mutton, boiled bacon and chicken. They drank a weak ale made from fermented barley. The hovels ("cots") in which they lived were single-roomed buildings of wattle and daub, with the bare earth as floor, roofs of straw or reed laid on branches, no windows and no chimney. All the furniture, utensils and clothing were home-made. But they were well organised. An open-air assembly, under the chairmanship of the Reeve, (a manorial official), met annually to appoint officers to look after the open fields and common pasture. They were rewarded by an extra allocation of strips for cultivation, or grazing.

Geoffrey de Mandeville was succeeded as lord of the manor by his son William, who was Constable of the Tower of London. He, in turn was succeeded, in about 1130, by his son Geoffrey — known in history as "the rebel". This title stemmed from his behaviour during the anarchic reign of King Stephen who, on the death of his uncle Henry I, had seized the crown from the rightful heir, his cousin Matilda.

Both sides sought the support of the Norman barons of whom Geoffrey de Mandeville was one of the most powerful, being Constable of the Tower and owning fortresses at Pleshy and Saffron Walden in Essex. Stephen created him Earl of Essex and granted him further estates; but when, in 1141, Matilda herself came to England and Stephen was for a time imprisoned, he transferred his allegiance to her and she confirmed him in the earldom of Essex and granted him more estates and privileges.

However, her cause faltered and, when Stephen was released, de Mandeville once more supported him in exchange for a pardon for his treason and further grants. He became sheriff and justice of Hertfordshire and of London and Middlesex, as well as of Essex, which gave him all the powers of administration and justice in the three counties. In 1142, he began to intrigue with Matilda and extracted more concessions from her. But this time he had overstepped the mark; jealous rivals accused him of treason, he was arrested and only escaped from being hanged by surrendering the Tower and his castles in Essex. He was then set free.

Supported by other nobles and their followers, he established himself in the Fens and headed a revolt. From his base at Fordham, he seized the Isle of Ely, and set up fortified headquarters at Ramsey Abbey. From there he and his followers went on the rampage, pillaging and burning Cambridge and smaller places. "Wicked men in their pride, and poor men in their misery, alike said that Christ and His saints slept", said the Anglo-Saxon chronicle. In August 1144, he attacked a fortified post of the king at Burwell, and was fatally wounded in the head. He died at Mildenhall and, since he had been excommunicated for his desecration and plunder of churches, it was not lawful to bury him. Some Knights Templars carried his body to their Old Temple in Holborn where it lay, encased in lead but unburied, for nearly twenty years.

Fortunately, Chippenham has never since had another such lord of the manor. Yet, in earlier more peaceful times, Geoffrey de Mandeville had founded Walden Priory (1136), endowed the first Chippenham church and given to the Prior of Walden the right of appointing the parish priest. It is not known when the church was built; folk legend says 1111 (the four ones) but it may have been even earlier. The round-headed doorway on the inside of the south wall and the walled-up windows in the north wall show that the old church was much smaller than the present one.

Geoffrey the Rebel's eldest son, Ernulf, was exiled and disinherited for bearing arms against the king, and his second son Geoffrey became the second Earl of Essex. King Henry II restored his possessions. In 1163, Geoffrey obtained absolution of his father from the Pope, and the body was buried in the New Temple in London. He died childless in 1166, and his brother William became third Earl of Essex and succeeded to his estates.

William de Mandeville was a very different man from his father. Before succeeding to his English earldom he had spent his life in France; subsequently he was frequently in attendance on Henry II and spent much of his time out of England. In 1177, he went on a crusade to the Holy Land with Philip, Count of Flanders, at whose court he had served as a young man and from whom he had received a knighthood. He took the Prior of Walden as his chaplain. He died, childless, at Rouen in November 1189, whither he had gone on business for the recently crowned King Richard I.

The de Mandeville estates passed to the de Say family, descendants of Geoffrey the Rebel's sister Beatrice and her husband William de Say. Chippenham, however, did not pass that way, for William de Mandeville had given the manor to the Knights Hospitallers in 1184. The church and its lands (extent unknown) belonged to the abbey of Walden; and the nunnery of Chicksands in Bedfordshire owned land which Geoffrey the Rebel's widow, Rohese, had given them for a grange — a gift confirmed by her sons, the second and third Earls of Essex.

The Chicksands Grange lay somewhere near the present junction of the A11 and A14 roads on the north-west side of the A11. Its lands were all around it at the south end of the village towards the heath. William de Mandeville took back some land nearer the village which his brother Geoffrey had added to the Chicksands grant, and gave them in exchange 116 acres of "newly cleared land" and 10 acres of arable, to which he added another 40 acres of arable and 10 acres of sheep pasture. The Grange already had pasture for 500 sheep and it is unlikely that the manor had less, so far more sheep were being kept than at the date of

Domesday Book. The de Mandevilles evidently brought considerable areas of heath land into cultivation, (marks of ridge and furrow were recorded 350 years later), but retained the better land nearer the village for their demesne.

Chapter 2

The Knights Hospitallers
12th to 15th centuries

The Order of the Hospital of St. John of Jerusalem was founded early in the 12th century, to help the sick and needy amongst pilgrims to the Holy Land. During the crusades, or holy wars, fought in the 12th and 13th centuries by the Christian powers of western Europe against Islam with the aim of restoring the Holy Land to Christian rule, the order became a military, as well as a religious one. Forced to leave the Holy Land after the fall of Acre in 1291, the Hospitallers moved their headquarters to Cyprus, subsequently to Rhodes and finally to Malta.

The headquarters of the Knights in England was situated at Clerkenwell in London. There were *preceptories* (known also as *commanderies*), or subordinate establishments, in other parts of the country, one of which was at Chippenham. The Chippenham preceptory was also the infirmary for sick Hospitallers for the whole priory in England. The Knights Hospitallers remained at Chippenham for three centuries, and their charters and records, together with the 1544 survey to which reference is made later, provide evidence of the layout of the village and its fields during this long period.

13th century

The centre of the village in the 13th century was not, as it is to-day, at the crossing of the High Street with the roads to Snailwell and Badlingham, but further south where "South Street" (a summer track of Icknield Way) crossed the High Street. The Hospitallers' hall and infirmary lay opposite the church, and the manor house was further south on the same side of the street. The population of Chippenham, as elsewhere, increased enormously during the 13th century and houses were built along the lane leading to Snailwell. The Hundred Rolls of 1279 show that there were 143 tenants of the manor which indicates a population of perhaps 650 to 700 — a figure exceeded only in the mid-nineteenth century.

The total acreage of the manor and abbey was 2121 acres (which included Chicksands land leased to the Hospital) comprising 769 acres of demesne land, 1135 acres tenanted by villeins and 217 by free tenants. There were 125 villeins of

5

Knights of St John. In monastic habit (above), in armour with tabard (below). *(By courtesy of the Museum of the Order of St John.)*

whom seventy held twelve to fifteen acres each, which was the smallest size of holding considered necessary to support a family; they paid a low rent and were liable for certain, though not very arduous, services. Four villeins held between seven and nine acres, paid higher rent and performed negligible services. The remaining fifty-one held only an acre or so, and presumably had to hire out their labour in order to earn a livelihood.

The "free" land was probably villein land enfranchised in the 12th century. This was never very extensive; the largest recorded freehold was ninety acres. Nevertheless, a good deal of buying and selling went on in the 13th century and much of the land was granted, leased back or sold to the abbey or the hospital, whose policy it evidently was to increase their land holdings. In 1279, there were eighteen free tenants of whom five were tenants of Walden Abbey and nine of the priory (including one who had four tenants of his own). Only two of these free tenants held as much as thirty acres, and eight held a dwelling alone or with only one or two acres.

The organisation of the preceptory is made clear in a report dated 1338. Though the parish church was owned by Walden Abbey (and the first vicars were probably Benedictine monks from the abbey), the Hospitallers had their own chapel in the church, as well as the quite separate chapel in the infirmary itself. This chapel was endowed by a number of grants in the form of chantries (endowments for priests to sing masses for the founder's soul) and gifts of land. The Hospitallers held parcels of land in other villages, notably in Ashley. King Henry III often stayed at Chippenham; in 1226, he granted a Monday market to the preceptory and, in 1234, he added to the grant an annual two-day fair at Michaelmas.

The preceptory budget for 1338 allowed for the preceptor, three brethren and two secular chaplains in the hall; the household staff and guests from time to time; and for seven brethren and three servants in the infirmary, with provision for other brethren according to the number of cases of sickness at the time. There were five *corrodarians*, or lay servants, who were maintained at the servants' table and earned a wage in addition. One of these was the *seneschal*, or chief steward, of the house; one was the porter and another probably the shoeing smith. There was also a *donat*, a lay brother who had given himself and his property to the Order, but had not taken vows; he ate at the brethren's table.

The general picture of Chippenham is of an overcrowded village of agricultural peasants, tilling the ground for their family food and, no doubt, serving in many capacities the domestic needs of the preceptory, which dominated the settlement.

The uniform of the Knights — a long black cloak with a white cross upon it — would have been a familiar sight to the villagers, and the comings and goings of the Knights, some directly from the wars in the Holy Land, must have given Chippenham a unique character among the villages of rural Cambridgeshire. No doubt the village boys fought their own battles between Knights (cops) and Saracens (robbers).

14th century

A dramatic fall in the population of the country occurred in the middle of the 14th century. There is evidence that the state of the village in 1334 had not changed much since 1279, but Poll Tax records in 1381 show only 204 adults over the age of fourteen, which indicates a population of only about three hundred. The principal cause of this fall was the Black Death, the outbreak of bubonic plague which reached England in 1348. It is estimated to have killed a third of the total inhabitants of the country; it struck at all levels of society, from the Archbishop of Canterbury himself downwards but most of all the working population. Two centuries later, when there were sixty village houses standing, sixty-four sites of former houses could be identified; the village was half its former size. Inevitably, there was a shortage of labour, which favoured tenants at the expense of landlords.

A Statute of Labourers in 1351, which tried to limit wages of farm labourers to what they were before the Black Death, was unpopular with both landlords, who were unable to compete for the labour available, and, of course, labourers; it proved impossible to enforce. It became difficult for landlords to enforce customary services; so leasehold tenancies became more common, the usual lease being ten years. Cottage tenancies, however, remained on a customary basis.

In 1381, the so-called Peasants Revolt broke out, as a result partly of the Statute of Labourers but chiefly of the poll tax, which was three times what it had been two years earlier and was not graded by rank. The revolt started in Kent, but there were serious risings in East Anglia. The abbey at Bury St. Edmunds was attacked, and at the same time property was stolen and cattle driven away from the Chippenham preceptory. The revolt in East Anglia was ruthlessly suppressed by the bishop of Norwich.

15th century

In 1446, a disastrous fire destroyed part of the village, and did much damage to the church. The village took a long time to recover, judging from the number of changes in tenancies recorded in the latter half of the century. The fire marked virtually the end of leasehold tenancy in the village; there was no attraction for tenants in short non-heritable leases. It was a buyers' market and, from that time on, the farmers of any sizeable amount of land held their tenancies on a lifelong or continuing basis, as *copyholders*. Thus it was that small holdings were combined and passed into the hands of a smaller number of men — a new rural class, the yeoman farmer.

There is not much information on the preceptory in the 15th century. A considerable reorganisation of the Order took place during the sojourn of the Knights at Rhodes, which affected the chief appointments in England and was felt in the preceptories. Certainly by quite early in the 16th century, the preceptory at Carbrooke, in Norfolk, had taken over the administration of the Chippenham preceptory and the infirmary had been closed. The manor was no more a religious house than any other owned by a community.

In 1540, the Hospital of St. John of Jerusalem was suppressed, and a new epoch in the history of Chippenham began, but before leaving the era of the Hospitallers, let us take a look at the church, as elsewhere the principal visible record of history in the village.

The small Norman church had been rebuilt in the Early English style. The chapel in the north aisle, with its painted roof, was the chapel of the Knights Hospitallers. Above the altar was a picture of the Virgin Mary (found embedded behind eight inches of stone and mortar in 1894). On the north wall was a painting of "St Michael weighing souls" (probably painted after the fire) and the coat of arms of Robert Botyll (or Bothell) prior of the great house of the Hospitallers at Clerkenwell from 1439 to 1469. Further west, was a painting of the martyrdom of St. Erasmus and, still further west, one of the giant St. Christopher carrying the child Christ on his shoulder. On the opposite south wall, was a painting of St. George slaying the dragon, and the king and queen watching from the city walls. All these paintings were described in detail in an article written for the Cambridge Antiquarian Society in 1886, a copy of which may be found in the church. In it the author said "much whitewash remains but it may be reasonably expected that many more subjects may be discovered." He regretted that a tablet had been fixed in the middle of the St. George picture. Rev. Barber, in his book of 1898, also describes the pictures and says that that of St. Christopher was found beneath a coating of plaster inscribed with post-Reformation black-letter texts, some of which had been allowed to remain. Now, nearly a hundred years later, no more pictures have been discovered, and the only pictures remaining are St. Christopher and St. Erasmus on the wall of the north aisle. Not a trace can be seen of St. George on the south aisle wall, which was evidently replastered at some time; and an attempt to renovate St. Michael in the 1980s resulted in its complete destruction. St. Christopher (without the black-letter texts) is in fairly good condition, and close observation will reveal the details of St. Erasmus. A casual visitor might miss it completely, so here is the description to help him:- "The saint, with his bishop's mitre, is laid on a bed, nude with the exception of a loin-cloth. Above are two figures on either side of a windlass, round which they are winding the bowels of the saint. Above, seated on a throne, is a royal personage, to whom two figures, in evident amazement, are pointing to the scene depicted above viz., the soul of the bishop being borne up to heaven in a napkin held by angels. The rays of heaven are shown in the upper part of the picture". The benches had carved poppy heads, no two exactly alike. A porch had been added to the south doorway. The tower had been completed and two bells hung — one dedicated to the Blessed Virgin, the other to the church's patroness St. Margaret. The rebuilding after the fire had been paid for by funds raised through promise of an indulgence which (in translation from the Latin) reads:-

St Margaret's Church. *(By courtesy of the artist, Barry Jelleyman.)*

"To all sons of Holy Mother Church to whom these present letters shall come, Thomas, by Divine permission Bishop of Ely, eternal health in the Lord. We consider that we are rendering welcome and moreover dutiful service so often as, by the alluring gifts of indulgences, we stir up the minds of the faithful with more readiness to works of piety and charity. Through, then, the boundless mercy of God . . . to all who are subject to our authority, who are truly penitent for their sins and have been confessed and are contrite, who of the goods which God has given to them shall have bestowed any welcome charitable assistance to the building or setting up of the Church of Chippenham in the diocese of Norwich, which was lately burnt by a sudden accident, by which it shall be possible to rebuild the said church anew, we by these presents, for so often as they shall do so, grant forty days of indulgence to last for a year only from the date of these presents. Given at our Manor of Downham, 12th October 1447, and the fourth year of our translation."

Chapter 3

The Reformation
16th century

By the end of the 15th century, the church had become extremely corrupt. Many priests were described as "ignorant and sensual men", greedy and dishonest. The sale of indulgences was only one of the more obvious scandals. Henry VIII's break with Rome was supported by a groundswell of anti-clericalism though its immediate cause was not a matter of doctrine, but of politics. The king was desperate for a male heir; his wife Catherine of Aragon had borne six children, including two sons, but only one daughter, Mary, had survived. Henry had fallen in love with Anne Boleyn and, in 1529, sought an annulment of his marriage from the Pope, which was refused. The "king's great matter" was eventually solved by legislation which brought about his marriage to Anne in 1533, and the break with Rome. Henry now became Supreme Head of the Church of England, and set about dissolving the monasteries — 374 lesser monasteries in 1536, and the 186 "great and solemn monasteries" in 1538-40. The monastery of Walden was granted to Lord Chancellor Audley.

At Chippenham, in 1547, the vicar (one presumes) removed the image of the Blessed Virgin in the north chapel in accordance with an Injunction. In 1549, an English Bible was placed in the church, chained for security; a chapter from the New Testament was read at matins on Sundays, and a chapter from the Old Testament at evensong. In the same year on Whit Sunday, the Communion service was said for the first time in English, instead of Latin; it continued to be called the Mass.

During her short reign (1553-8) Mary attempted to restore the Catholic faith and to re-impose the authority of the Pope, but failed. Reformers were persecuted — some burnt — the Latin service restored, and the English Prayer book forbidden. But in Elizabeth's reign (1558-1603) it was the papists' turn to suffer persecution — and execution. The English prayer book came back, and by the end of her reign, most of the scandalous practices had disappeared and the priesthood numbered many scholars in its ranks.

These changes seem to have had little effect on most parish priests, who almost all conformed to changes in doctrine and ritual. One vicar of Chippenham,

Robert Taverham, appointed in 1549, was deprived of the living soon after Mary's accession — perhaps because he had married; but Robert Webster, appointed during Mary's reign, remained as vicar for thirty years.

Reference in wills to the Virgin Mary are common up to the time of Elizabeth, though it is not possible to say whether they truly reflected the beliefs of the testator or of the vicar, who might well have written them. Nicholas Allen, vicar from 1587 to 1633, was a teaching minister and strongly Protestant; wills witnessed (and probably written) by him reflect this in their reference to Christ alone as the True Saviour. Most of the successful yeoman farmers of the following century wrote dedicatory clauses in their wills in the Protestant style.

The lordship of Chippenham (along with other abbey lands) was given to Sir Edward North (b. 1496?), treasurer of the Court of Augmentations (which administered the revenues from Crown lands acquired from the monasteries) and one of the MPs for Cambridgeshire. About 1530, he had married a rich widow and was able to purchase an estate at Kirtling. In 1554, he was created a baron as the first Lord North of Kirtling. He died in 1564 and was buried there; he was evidently an absentee landlord so far as Chippenham was concerned.

The leading man in the village was the demesne lessee, Thomas Bowles. His father had obtained the demesne farm and its stock for forty six years from 1529, was also the farmer of Chicksands Grange, and had acquired the property in Chippenham of Walden Abbey from the Audley family to whom the monastery had been granted. He had also bought, some years before the suppression of the hospital, the valuable furniture of its church (the sale may have been a result of the pressing need for money to continue the Knights' war against the Turks). In the year 1544, when a land survey of Chippenham was made, Thomas Bowles was farming more than one-fifth of the open fields, and also held five other farms. He acquired the patronage in 1549, and appointed three vicars between then and 1557. There is an unsolved riddle regarding this man. A man of the same name was a trusted servant of the Duke of Norfolk, who was beheaded in 1572 and his property confiscated. One of his three properties, Tendring Hall, Stoke-by-Nayland, was given by Queen Elizabeth to Thomas Revett. At the same time, Revett succeeded Bowles as owner of Chippenham. Were the two Bowles one and the same man, who forfeited his property in the shadow of his master?

Thomas Revett entertained Queen Elizabeth at Chippenham on 31 August 1578, during one of her "Progresses" through East Anglia; she went on to Lord North's at Kirtling. While at Chippenham, "all things were well and in very good order, and meate liberally spent". The queen evidently thought so, for she knighted Revett on the spot. Sir Thomas died in 1582, at the age of sixty-two, and was buried at Chippenham. There is a handsome monument to him in the chancel of the church, which shows him kneeling on the left, his two wives on the right, and four daughters in front. The inscription gives the names of all these ladies.

In his will, Sir Thomas left £2-12-0 per annum together with the dividends

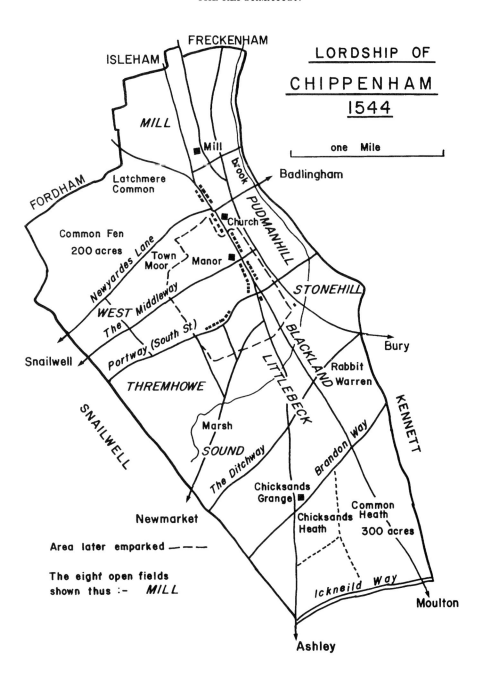

Adapted from a map based on Dr M Spufford's study of the 1544 survey, by kind permission.

from £59-6-5 to provide thirteen penny loaves of good sweet bread to be distributed to thirteen poor in his name every Sunday weekly for ever before the end of morning prayer. He left no male heir, and the Chippenham lordship passed to Sir William Russell, husband of his granddaughter Elizabeth Gerard (or Jarrett).

The survey of 1544 shows that forty-five men held (or had recently held) land in the village, that half the tenants held a house only or a house and one or two acres, and that at least fifteen householders were landless. In 1279, only two out of 143 tenants held 30 acres or more; in 1544, more than a third of the tenants had farms of this size or above and the largest copyholder held over a hundred acres. In 1279, the tenants' holdings had provided bare subsistence to an overpopulated community; in 1544, the community was half the size, a number of large farmers were much better off but the landless were probably poorer. There were sixty three houses, with a resident population between 250 and 300.

60% of the lordship was arable, lying in eight open fields. Strip farming was still the pattern; the size of strips varied. Three tenants each holding fifty-six acres had 120, 111 and 89 strips, so the average strip was about half an acre. Land on poorer soil was tending to go out of cultivation; the former Chicksands arable was now pure heath. The heath and fen together amounted to eight hundred acres, but only five hundred of this was common to tenants — two hundred acres of fen and three hundred of heath. Tenants also had common rights over small areas of demesne pasture at certain seasons. Sir Thomas Revett, it seems, enclosed the fen (presumably denying the right of digging turf for fuel, which was so precious to the poor).

Although the arable area had been reduced, the farmers in the 16th century attempted to increase their sheep flocks. In 1518, the farmer of the Walden Abbey land, which had about forty acres of fallow, was ordered to reduce his flock from at least two hundred to a hundred and twenty; and the farmer of Chicksands, with two hundred acres of fallow, from at least four hundred to two hundred. In 1544, Thomas Bowles was running at least two thousand sheep and, according to tenants, was trying to deny their rights to pasture their own sheep. It seems that this was successful and that the folding of sheep on the cornfields became the monopoly of the manor.

Even if they could not keep sheep, the farmers did keep cattle and pigs, for which they still held common rights. Some of those with the larger farms had horses for their ploughs.

Chapter 4

The Russells, Baronets of Chippenham
17th century

The issues which led, in the 17th century, to civil war, the execution of King Charles I in 1649 and the Commonwealth (1649-60), were both constitutional and religious. The constitutional issue concerned the determination of Parliament to restrict the royal prerogative and to assert its right to vote taxes. The religious issue arose from the growth of Puritanism, which embraced a number of doctrines with the common aim of opposing the episcopacy of the reformed English church, and sought to rid it of elements considered still to be Roman Catholic, or "superstitious". Puritanism came to be increasingly identified with Parliament, while King Charles was an Arminian, opposed to Calvinist doctrines upon which Puritanism was based, and widely suspected of being at heart a Roman Catholic. He had, moreover, married Henrietta Maria of France, a staunch Roman Catholic

The Russells, Baronets of Chippenham, owned the village for a century. Sir William, the first baronet, had three wives, of whom Elizabeth Gerard was the second. By her, he had seven sons and three daughters. These supported different sides during the struggles between King and Parliament. Sir William was a director of the East India Company, and had traded as an adventurer with the Muscovy Company. He became Treasurer of the Navy in 1618, and was created Baronet in 1630. He was a man of considerable wealth who frequently lent money to the government of Charles I, and he remained loyal to the king. In 1640, he resigned the patronage of Chippenham to his eldest son Francis, realising perhaps that it would be useless to appoint a Royalist clergyman. He died in 1654, and was buried at Chippenham.

Charles I had visited him at Chippenham. A year after his defeat at the Battle of Naseby (June 1645), the king had placed himself in the hands of the Scottish army at Newark, but the Scots sold him to the parliamentarians. He was taken to Holdenby House in Northamptonshire from which he was removed, a few months later, by the army. During months of fruitless attempts to reach a settlement, Charles was moved around to suit the convenience of the army. In June 1647 he was at Newmarket, where he was well treated. He was able to hold court at the small house fitted up for him. He always had company at meals and enjoyed riding, racing and hunting on the heath. He also played bowls with Sir William Russell at the Hall, and there is a record of his meeting with an emissary from parliament on the lawn.

Sir William's eldest son Francis, the second baronet, allied himself with Cromwell. He had fourteen children (of whom several died in infancy); in 1653, his eldest daughter Elizabeth married Oliver Cromwell's son Henry, Lord Deputy of Ireland. They often stayed at the Hall and Oliver Cromwell himself — a local man, MP for Cambridge city, with a house at Ely — must certainly have visited Chippenham. Francis Russell was a Colonel of Foot in the army of the Eastern Association early in the civil war, and it seems likely that some Chippenham villagers would also have served in it and in the New Model Army later; Robert Tebbutt, who died in 1668, left a sword, bandoliers and muskets hanging in his hall.

In 1640, Francis Russell had presented Dr. John Gauden (1605-62), his brother-in-law, as vicar of Chippenham. Gauden had, earlier, been tutor to two sons of Sir William Russell [it is not clear whether Francis was one of them] and had married his daughter Elizabeth. He provides a good example of what must have been a common problem, in those troubled times, of reconciling family ties, political inclinations and religious beliefs. The DNB says that he "maintained an ambiguous position, retaining his preferments and conforming to presbyterianism, though publishing books on behalf of the Church of England". He himself said that he was "for regulating, not rooting out, episcopacy". Amongst his writings, he claimed authorship of the *Eicon Basilike — the Pourtraiture of his Sacred Majestie in His Solitudes and Sufferings*. Historical opinion was for long divided as to whether these purported meditations of the king were, in fact, the king's own or whether they were written, at least in part, by Gauden; the weight of evidence appears to be strongly in support of Gauden's authorship. While vicar of Chippenham, he was also chaplain to Robert Rich, second earl of Warwick, a man of strongly parliamentary sympathies. In 1642, through Warwick's influence, he was promoted to the deanery of Bocking in Essex; but on the restoration of Charles II in 1660, he became chaplain to the king and was appointed bishop of Exeter and later of Worcester. Though he left no mark on the village during his short stay, he was one of the many interesting men who have a place in the history of Chippenham.

Two more church bells were hung early in this century, one inscribed "John Draper [of Thetford] made me. 1601", and the fine tenor bell inscribed "John Draper made me. 1621".

A Suffolk puritan, William Dowsing, was appointed by parliament to destroy all subjects considered to be superstitious in Cambridgeshire and Suffolk. He has been described by a local historian as "a portentous clown . . . Everything appeared superstitious to his narrow, ill-informed mind". He visited Chippenham on 23 March 1643 and recorded that he had destroyed "Two superstitious pictures: *orate pro animabus* [pray for the soul] and divers other superstitious ones in the window". It is not known which window this was, but whatever stained glass there was in the church was destroyed, and the frescoes were covered in whitewash. Little is known about George Warren, the vicar during this period, nor of the exact date when he was succeeded by Richard Parr, a Puritan. After the restoration of Charles II in 1660, an Act of Uniformity was passed laying down that church services were to be conducted according to a revised prayer book. Many clergy who refused to comply were forced to resign their livings, and Richard Parr was one of them. He ended his days with Henry Cromwell at Spinney Abbey, Wicken.

It happened by chance that shortly after Mr. Parr had resigned in 1662, Isaac Archer, recently ordained at the age of twenty one, was sent to preach at Chippenham. He was well received by Sir Francis Russell who promptly offered him the living. Archer was vicar of Chippenham for twenty-five years. During this time he was often absent for quite long periods serving and preaching in other parishes and seeking to practise the barely conforming type of worship he favoured. He was very sympathetic to Non-conformists. He was an inspiring preacher (though he had to choose his words carefully because of a bad stammer), and the Non-conformists would come to church to hear him, though rejecting the liturgy. There were said to be twenty Quakers in the village and, in 1672, Quakers, Congregationalists and Presbyterians all met in the village, the Presbyterians actually meeting at the vicarage. Only a few had to answer charges of holding unsound doctrines or withholding tithes, the most conspicuous being John Tetsall and his wife, who were obstinate Quakers.

We are fortunate that Archer left a detailed Diary [Suffolk Records Society xxxvi, 1994], describing the Hall and the village, as well as his own spiritual struggles.

Sir Francis Russell died in 1664, and was buried at Chippenham. His eldest son John, third baronet, aged thirty one, had distinguished himself in the parliamentary army at the battle of Marston Moor and in Ireland. He had cemented the existing family ties by marrying in 1659 Oliver Cromwell's fourth daughter Frances, a widow. (In 1657, she had married Robert Rich, grandson and heir of the second earl of Warwick, but he had died the following year, just two months before the earl himself). The Russell family fortunes were in a poor state; Sir John was often away from Chippenham attempting to save his estate from complete collapse, and he tried unsuccessfully to sell it in 1667. He died in 1669 at the early age of thirty six, and was buried at Chippenham. He and his wife left a long and tender correspondence, written during his absences. [*Hist.* Mss. Commission, *Report on the Manuscripts of Mrs. Frankland Russell-Astley*, London 1900]

During his short term as lord of the manor, Chippenham Hall was occupied during his frequent absences by a number of gentry families, attracted by the proximity of Newmarket, which was a centre not only of horse-racing but also of hunting, cock-fighting, gaming and card-playing; moreover the king had a small palace in the town. Archer was, on one occasion, badgered into taking part in the activities at the Hall and nearly lost an eye fencing, but he disapproved strongly of the bad example being set to the villagers. He preached against drunkenness with some success, and was very concerned that some of the gentry from the Hall actually patronised the alehouse and that the village constable would not assist him against those who frequented it, illegally, on Sundays. Disheartened he left, in 1671, for another parish, but did not get on well with the gentry there and returned to Chippenham in 1673.

In his will, Sir John Russell directed that the estate should be sold, and a smaller estate purchased for his son and heir. Sir William, the fourth baronet, was a boy not yet in his teens, and the estate was administered by trustees on behalf of him and his mother. Lady Frances, however got increasingly into debt and Sir William proved very extravagant; by the middle 1680s it had become imperative to sell the Chippenham estate. Archer left early in 1688 having obtained the living of Mildenhall, and, in May, the whole of the Russell estates in Cambridgeshire were sold to Admiral Edward Russell (who was not a close relation, but may have been a distant one) for £16,270. After all their debts had been paid, Lady Frances and Sir William received less than a quarter of this money.

Some evidence of the status of village residents in the late 17th century can be gleaned from records of the Hearth Tax. This tax was introduced as a means of raising money after the restoration of Charles II. It was collected twice a year at the rate of one shilling for each hearth. It has been estimated that since the survey of 1544, the population of the village had risen by about 20%, but available land was passing into fewer and fewer hands. On Lady Day 1647, of seventy-two houses listed (of which nine or ten may have been in Badlingham), thirty-five were those of the average labourer with one or two hearths, and twenty-four those of yeomen or prosperous craftsmen with three or more hearths; the Hall itself had thirty-four hearths. The poor, who did not pay parish rates, were exempt. In houses with one hearth, the hall served as both living room and kitchen, while a two-hearth house would have separate hall and kitchen. One yeoman's house of this time had a hall and parlour with chambers above them and garrets, dairy, cheese chamber and cellars. This three storey house may, possibly, have been the present-day Church Farmhouse. In 1679 one of the yeoman farmers, Thomas Delamore, left 16¾ acres of land for the benefit of the poor of the village.

Chapter 5

Admiral Russell, Lord Orford emparks the village

After the execution of Charles I, his elder son was crowned as King Charles II in Scotland. In 1651, he invaded England at the head of a Scottish army but was defeated by Oliver Cromwell at Worcester. He fled to the continent and lived in exile for nine years, until his restoration as king in 1660. He married a Portuguese princess by whom he had no children, though he had plenty of illegitimate offspring. In the late 1660s, his brother and heir James, Duke of York, became a Roman Catholic and later married a second wife who was a Catholic but, despite attempts to exclude him from the succession, he became king on the death of Charles II in 1685. Their sister, Mary, married the Protestant Dutchman, William of Orange; her son William (later King William III) married his first cousin Mary (later Queen Mary II), elder daughter of James II by his first wife Anne Hyde. William and Mary were staunch Protestants. The scene was set for another conflict of loyalties.

Edward Russell was born in 1653, a nephew of the fifth Earl (later the first Duke) of Bedford. He entered the Navy, probably in 1667. He proved such a good seaman that, only five years later, his Commander-in-Chief, James Duke of York, promoted him to Captain in recognition of his service against the Dutch at the Battle of Solebay, and gave him the command of a 42-gun ship. He was only eighteen years old; he served as Captain for the next ten years. In 1683, his first cousin Lord William Russell (to whom he was devoted), one of those who supported attempts to exclude James from the succession, was executed for high treason. He immediately resigned his commission and his post in the Duke of York's household. When the Duke came to the throne as James II in 1685, Edward Russell (for political rather than religious reasons) joined those who set out to replace him by William of Orange, and became the active messenger between the conspirators in England and William in Holland. He was one of the seven prominent persons who, in 1688, signed a letter inviting William to come with an army to "protect the liberties of England" and he travelled with the invasion fleet. After the landing at Torbay (the "Glorious Revolution"), he accompanied William on his march to London. James II fled to France, William

Edward Russell, Earl of Orford. *(By courtesy of National Maritime Museum.)*

and Mary were crowned, and England and Holland declared war on France.

In 1689, Russell was given the lucrative post of Treasurer of the Navy and was appointed Admiral of the Blue Squadron under the Commander-in-Chief of the Anglo-Dutch fleet, the Earl of Torrington. He also became a Privy Councillor and a member of William's inner cabinet. In July 1690, Torrington was ordered to sea, with an inferior fleet, to fight the French and was defeated at the Battle of Beachy Head. Though he was Admiral of the Blue, Russell remained in London because William had nominated him as one of the Lords Justices to advise Mary during his absence with the army in Flanders. After the battle, Torrington was court-martialled for exercising undue caution and, though acquitted, he was superseded. Russell, when offered the command, at first refused it but was persuaded to accept it after attempts to find a trio of Admirals to share a joint command had failed.

The Battle of Barfleur — La Hougue ("La Hogue")

In May 1692, the French were planning an invasion of England to be led by James in person, in the belief that many English naval officers would place their attachment to the Jacobite cause before their loyalty to their country. Admiral Tourville, in command of a French fleet, received personal orders from King Louis to seek and engage the English fleet even if he was inferior in numbers; so many of the English were expected to desert that the consequent demoralisation would ensure a French victory. Tourville sailed from Brest with forty four ships of the line, without waiting for a Toulon squadron which was on its way to reinforce him. Russell left Portsmouth with an Anglo-Dutch fleet of eighty-two ships and steered across the channel towards the Cotentin peninsula. On the morning of 19 May, the fleets were in sight of one another. The wind was from the south west and Tourville, to windward of the Anglo-Dutch fleet, closed to engage. The battle went on all day. Tourville's flagship the *Soleil Royal* was closely engaged by Russell's flagship *Britannia*, and so crippled in masts and rigging that she had to be towed out of the line; but in the day's fighting not a single French ship had struck her colours or been sunk, which says much for the spirit of Tourville's fleet. By four o'clock, however, the French centre and rear ships were enveloped by the English fleet with a two-to-one superiority, and an English victory seemed inevitable. But the wind dropped, a dense fog came on and the fleets anchored. Later a light easterly wind sprung up and the fog lifted a little. The French beat an honourable retreat, pursued by the English throughout the night and the next day. The main retreat was towards the Channel Islands and twenty ships managed to escape, with a favourable current, through the dangerous Race of Alderney. Before the remaining fifteen could do so, the tide changed and they drifted back to the eastward. Three ran themselves aground at Cherbourg (at that time an open roadstead) and twelve, including the *Soleil Royal*, in the bay at St. Vaast-la Hougue. Those at Cherbourg were burnt by sailors from boats of Vice

Admiral Delaval's squadron; now followed the decisive action of the Battle of La Hogue. The English ships were unable to close the shore owing to the shallow water, so Russell sent in the boats of the fleet under Vice Admiral Rooke, and the sailors burnt the whole twelve as well as some transports. The spectacular destruction of these ships when the fires reached the magazines was witnessed by the whole of the invasion army and a number of important personages, and the moral effect proved fatal to the French navy. Sir Winston Churchill, in later days, called the battle "the Trafalgar of the Seventeenth Century". James, who was himself present, is reputed to have exclaimed, in the excitement of the occasion, "See my brave English sailors!"

Despite the decisiveness of the victory, the politicians expected Russell to destroy the remainder of the fleet which had taken refuge at St. Malo. Russell deemed this impracticable, and he was removed from his command. An historian of the day wrote "The bold advance of Tourville with the tardiness of Russell, raised doubts and anxieties in many of the English captains. They looked around, to see when their own officers were to rise up against them, or when the ships next to theirs were to quit the line and sail over to their enemies". In the circumstances of the time, doubts about loyalty and accusations of treason were common currency; but none of this actually happened. The emissary who attempted to suborn a number of Whigs to James's cause had no success with Russell — "he gave warning that, as he was an officer and an Englishman, it behoved him to fire on the first French ship that he met, although he saw James upon the quarterdeck".

During the year after the Battle of La Hogue, English shipping suffered severe losses at the hands of the French, and late in the year Russell was reinstated in his command and also appointed First Lord of the Admiralty (he was still Treasurer of the Navy and of the Royal Household). In 1695, with his fleet in the Mediterranean, he effectively prevented the French from attacking Barcelona and the coast of Spain. This was the end of Russell's service afloat, but he remained at the Admiralty until 1699. He had played an important part in politics, as MP for Cambridgeshire from 1695 and in the House of Lords from May 1697 when he was raised to the peerage as Baron Shingey, Viscount Barfleur and Earl of Orford, and was one of the four "Lords of the Junto" which controlled the Whig party.

In 1701, he was impeached by the Tory majority in the House of Commons together with Lords Somers, Halifax and Jersey, the particular charge against Orford being that he had sold ships and applied the proceeds to his own use, and taken grants from the king. He denied the first charge, but admitted having received a gift of £10,000 from the king after his dismissal in 1692. According to John Evelyn the diarist, "The Lords without granting a free Conference to the Commons, how the Trials of the Impeached Lords should be managed, tryed and acquitted them, the Commons refusing to appear, because the Lords began to try those Impeached peers, against whom they had the least to object, whilst the

Commons (whose part it was to do so) insisted to have the L. Summers tryed first". Lord Orford was certainly a very rich man and this was not the only occasion on which he was accused of corruption. However, he came from the wealthy Bedford family and had received a good inheritance at an early age. Moreover, when charged with profiting himself from the victualling of the fleet in 1694-5, he was able to show that he had spent less than the official allowance.

He became First Lord of the Admiralty again in 1709-10 in Queen Anne's reign, and from 1714-17 under George I. He entertained the king at Chippenham on 4 October 1717. He became Lord Lieutenant of Cambridgeshire in 1714. He married a cousin Lady Margaret Russell, daughter of the first Duke of Bedford, who died in 1702. They had no children so, when he died on 26 November 1727, his titles became extinct. He and his wife were buried in the Russell family vault at Chenies, Buckinghamshire. (Robert Walpole, who was Prime Minister from 1721 to 1742, was a protégé of Russell and, when offered a peerage, took the title of Lord Orford as a compliment to his friend).

In 1696, Russell had bought most of the remaining copyhold land in Chippenham which was held by only five men. In 1702, he addressed a letter to William III which read "Your petitioner has a seat called Chippenham Hall . . . about which he is desirous to make a Park". This park was to include the bottom end of the High Street south of the manor and the whole of South Street.

Chippenham Hall as it is today (re-built c.1890.)

It involved the loss of at least twenty five houses. A licence was obtained to block roads from Snailwell to Chippenham and from Newmarket to Mildenhall, alternative routes being provided on estate land. The "Inhabitants and Owners" of Chippenham — eleven in number — agreed to relinquish their rights of common on such land as was emparked, and received in compensation rights of common for cattle, but not sheep, on all the Lammas land in the village and on part of the fen occupied by the demesne lessee. At least fourteen cottages were built on "New Street", or Vicarage Lane, the road to Badlingham. In 1712, Heber Lands surveyed the estate and produced a magnificent illustrated map showing all the buildings together with the acreage and names of the holders of every strip in the open fields. The map shows a maximum of fifty houses (it is not possible in all cases to tell whether a building was a single or two houses), and it seems certain that the emparking must have caused some villagers to leave. The map shows clearly the line of the former South Street, with only two small buildings on it. There are still footings where the old High and South Streets ran in the Park.

The map shows that, in 1712, three tenants — John Tetsal, Thomas Elliott and Ambrose Davy — farmed more than 250 acres each (about 1000 acres among them out of the total arable land of 1600 acres), four farmed 100 to 150 acres, two farmed about 60 acres, one 15 acres and eight more less than 5 acres — eighteen landholders in all. Other villagers had a house or cottage only. The open fields were still farmed on the strip system but the acreages of single strips were, in many cases, much larger than in earlier years, amounting almost to individual (though not enclosed) fields.

John Tetsal's land was in 156 strips mainly in the northern fields of the village. Thomas Elliott farmed many fewer strips in the open fields, but held some sizeable acreages, comparable to those of modern fields. The map shows that he farmed the whole of the glebe land; he also farmed the area between the road to Fordham and the Fen. Ambrose Davy had the "New Farm", later named La Hogue Hall, the first farmstead to be built outside the village, and also former Chicksands and demesne land to the south of the village — virtually all the land to the south of the Park, except the common grazing on the heath.

Chippenham Hall is said to have been built to the design of Inigo Jones (who died in 1652), but there does not seem to be any positive evidence of this. Lord Orford now enlarged the hall, built the handsome stable block and laid out the park and gardens in the formal Dutch manner popular at the time. In 1698, Celia Fiennes in the course of *My Great Journey to Newcastle and to Cornwall*, visited Lord Orford and described the house in her diary, and a very splendid house it was:-

*"I passed by a village or two and in a mile of Lord Orfords house I Enter
Cambridgeshire, which stands 3 mile from Newmarket . . . A Coach yard and stables
in the middle of which is a large gate into ye ground, and built over with a high
lanthorn where hangs the Clock and bell: this stands higher than the house like a tower:
ye house being a flatt Roofe leaded and railed round full of chimneys, but this tower I*

saw 10 mile off. All ye offices built round the Court very handsome. The hall is very noble paved with free stane . . . its hung with pictures att full proportion of ye Royal family all in their Coronation Robes, from Charles the first to his Majesty with ye Queen also.

"*In ye best drawing roome was a very rich hanging gold and silver and a little scarlet, mostly tissue and brocade of gold and silver and border of green damaske round it, ye window curtain ye same green damaske and doore Curtains. Ye same was in another drawing room which was for my Lord. The dining room had this looking glass on ye top peers between the three windows: it was from ye top to ye bottom 2 pannells in breadth and 7 in length so it shews one from top to toe. The roomes were all well wanscoated and hung and there was ye finest Carv'd wood in fruitages, herbages,*

Chippenham Park. The stable clock and lantern.

gumms, beastes, fowles &c. very thin and fine all in white wood without paint or varnish. Ye several sorts of things thus Carv'd were Exceeding naturall all round. The Chimney pieces and ye sconces stand on Each side the Chimney, and the glasses in those Chambers where were loose Looking-glasses which were with fine Carv'd head and frames some of the naturall wood others Gilt but they were ye largest Looking-glasses which I ever saw. There was a great flower pott Gilt Each side the Chimney in the dineing roome for to sett trees in. Ye great curiosity of this wood Carving about ye Doores Chimneys and sconces together with ye great Looking-glass pannells is much talked of and is ye finest and most in quantety and numbers that's to be seen anywhere . . . Ye common Roomes are all new Convenient and neate with Double doores lined to prevent noises. Ye Stairs case is wanscoated very noble fine pictures there is ye battle at la Hogue a large sea piece with an inscription of ye admirals valour when ye great ship ye sunn was burnt and mightily valued by ye ffrench King".

The staff required to run the estate is recorded in Orford's household expenses account for 1717/18. He employed eighteen men, two boys and eight female staff. The wages bill for the male staff was £233, for the female staff £45 and £71.8.6 was paid for "liveries" — a total of £349.8.6. The gardener was the best paid at

25

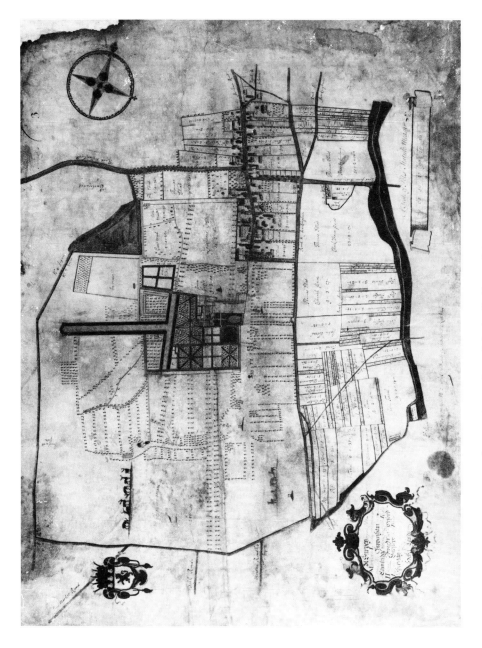

Centre sheet of Lord Orford's Estate Map, 1712.

£40 a year, the receiver of rents, cook (male) and park-keeper each got £25 a year.

Lord Orford also had three other houses. His town house was in Covent Garden, and a country house in the grounds of Chelsea Hospital. The third was a small manor house at Ugley, Essex, given to him by King William. He never lived there, but it was a convenient half-way house for him and his guests on the two-day travel by coach from London to Chippenham.

According to an article in *Household Words* (edited by Charles Dickens) in 1853, Lord Orford celebrated the victory of La Hogue at Chippenham with the largest bowl of punch ever made. A cistern was made into which were poured:- 4 hogsheads of brandy, 8 hogsheads of water, 25000 lemons, 13cwt of sugar, 5 lbs. of grated nutmeg, 300 toasted biscuits, and a pipe of dry mountain Malaga wine. "In this lake of liquor floated a small boat with a steady boat's crew. These filled for all comers, and more than 6000 persons partook of the admiral's mixture. The cistern or bowl was empty long before morning". This was written 160 years after the event and the story may have improved with each telling during that time, but it seems to ring true to Orford's character. He also planted two lines of lime trees, one on each side of the park, representing the positions of the opposing fleets at the battle of La Hogue.

Lord Orford's principal benefaction to the village was the school. The vicar of Chippenham and chaplain to Lord Orford (and later to George II) was Samuel Knight (1674-1746), a distinguished man, a pioneer of education and district secretary of the Society for the Promotion of Christian Knowledge (founded in 1699), and also the biographer of Dean Colet and Erasmus. In July 1708, he wrote in a letter, "My Lord Orford hath bought a house, which he designs very suddenly to fit up, or rather rebuild, for a school house." This building, on the site of the Knights' preceptory opposite the church, was to remain the village school for more than two and a half centuries. In his will, Lord Orford left £10 a year for "poor Housekeepers" and £20 a year for a schoolmaster provided that he did not teach Latin. It was his intention that English, reading, writing and arithmetic should be taught, and that every village child should attend.

The church was well maintained under Samuel Knight. Lord Orford presented a chalice and paten, and William Cole (of whom more hereafter) wrote in 1745 — "Over ye south door is wrote 'This church was beautified AD 1707. Stephen Tetsall, James Jarold, Churchwardens'". A good parochial library, provided by the SPCK, was held in the church. A fifth bell was hung which is inscribed "T. Newman [of Norwich] made me. 1703". "J. Jarrold S. Tetsall. C.W." Samuel Knight was succeeded by William Robinson, and became Rector of Bluntisham, where he was buried. His wife died in 1719, soon after giving birth to their only child; she was buried at Chippenham and there is a memorial tablet on the north wall of the chancel.

Chapter 6

From emparking to enclosure
18th century

At Lord Orford's death, Chippenham passed to his great-niece Letitia, wife of Samuel Sandys, a descendant of an Archbishop of York in Elizabeth's reign. Sandys was appointed Chancellor and Under Treasurer of the Exchequer in 1741, and was elevated to the peerage as Baron Sandys of Ombersley (Worcs) in 1743.

The vicar, at this time, was Clement Tookie LL.D who had been appointed in about 1720, and held the living for nearly thirty years. He was very meticulous in keeping the Parish Register, in which he recorded a list of all the vicars and patrons from the year 1311, copies of the Rivett and Orford wills, and a list of the twenty-one pieces of glebe land (which amounted, in all, to fifteen acres). He made and displayed in the church two boards recording the parochial charities. He died in 1748 and was buried at the west end of the church; there is a slab in the tower floor which records that he was also Rector of Worlington and Prebendary of Ely. He was succeeded by his son, Clement Tookie the second, who was vicar for forty-six years, so that the combined incumbencies of father and son lasted for three quarters of the century. The younger Tookie died, at the age of eight-one in 1794.

There is a very full description of the church at the time that Lord Sandys was lord of the manor by William Cole (1714-82). Cole was a Cambridge antiquary who left nearly a hundred folio volumes in his own handwriting, with drawings of monuments and armorial bearings, which are now in the British Library under the title *Parochial Antiquities of Cambridgeshire*. The church at Chippenham, which he visited on 30 May 1745, is described in Additional MSS.5807.

His text is illustrated with sketches of the outside of the church, of the Rivett and Hanna Knight monuments, and of two hatchments depicting the arms of the Earl and Countess of Orford which were hung between these two monuments. There is also a sketch of the painted wooden memorial, which he "forgot to ask the vicar about" and which has never been identified. The diamond-shaped marble memorials to young Tookies and others, at the west end of the north aisle, were at that time enclosed; over the north door was written "God save Queen Anne".

"A very neat and light screen" divided the nave from the chancel, on top of which were devices for the Kings of England, France, Ireland and Scotland and, between them, ovals containing letters which read "Carole Vive Diu" on the nave side and "Carole Vive Deo" on the chancel side.

A canopied three-decker pulpit stood where the present pulpit stands (it was pulled down in 1885.) Lord Sandy's pew was opposite it in the south aisle, and was entered through a door (where the organ now stands) from the chapel at the east end of the aisle.

"The beautiful neat marble font stands in ye middle isle bet. ye N and S doors — of fine black and gold veined marble — it is rail'd with iron to prevent any rude Jostle against it, which might throw it down: it is exactly like ye fonts for Holy Water wh. stand at ye entrance into ye churches abroad." Unfortunately, it was not really suitable as a font as it had no drain to empty the water, and it was in due course broken by the "rude Jostle".

"A neat library" was stationed at the west end of the south aisle, separated by wainscoting. Cole forgot to ask Tookie who had left it; it was presumably the SPCK library of Samuel Knight.

Cole commented that the school opposite the church was "elegant and beautiful", and that there were the arms of Lord Orford over the door.

While the Tookies provided continuity in the village through most of the 18th century, ownership of the estate changed hands several times. About 1745, Lord Sandys built the lodges and arch at the south end of the park, which form the gateway to the coach road to Newmarket. The sculpture of Hope above the arch was added by John Tharp about 1800. Lord Sandys sold the estate, in 1749, to George Montgomerie (1712-66), some time High Sheriff of Cambridge and Huntingdon, and M.P. for Ipswich.

George Montgomerie's daughter, Kate, married Crisp Molyneux of Garboldisham Hall, Norfolk; and Montgomerie left the Chippenham estate to his grandson George Molyneux (b. 1761) on attaining the age of twenty-one. He also left "£20 to Poor of Chippenham and £100 to Poor Housekeepers and Industrious Persons of the parish, who do not receive alms", to be distributed by the Vicar, Churchwardens and Overseers of the Poor. He died in 1766, and Crisp Molyneux administered the estate until his son came of age in 1782. George Molyneux assumed the name of Montgomerie in accordance with his grandfather's will. He was also heir to his father's extensive estate at Garboldisham and, in 1787, he sold the Chippenham estate to Drummond Smith, a London man.

An advertisement for the estate in 1783 had described the Park in considerable detail including "A most superb magnificent capital Mansion House consisting of rooms of every description, and all convenient offices detached, with a reservoir of water supplying the whole house", It added "There has been upwards of 1200£ laid out within the last four years in improvements upon the premises, which are now in compleat repair". Drummond Smith was lord of the manor for little more than four years. During that time, he pulled down a large part of the mansion, reducing it to the size of a modest shooting or hunting lodge. A sketch shows a very simple centre facade of two storeys in the Georgian style, with the office wings, and is labelled Chippenham Lodge. One wonders what was the reason for this act of destruction; the fact that he reduced the size of the house so drastically and then kept the estate for only four years suggests that he had financial problems, and that his purchase of the estate may have been a speculation which did not work out as he had hoped. But before he left Chippenham, the biggest change in the village took place since the time of its emparkment by Lord Orford.

Widespread changes in agriculture took place in the 18th century. For centuries past, wheat rye and beans had been sown in the autumn, and barley oats and peas in the spring, and about a third of the land was left fallow. Higher yields from crops were mainly dependent on animal manure. Now, the introduction of new winter feed crops such as clover and turnips as part of three-year rotations, enabled farmers to keep more livestock, and hence obtain more animal manure. New agricultural implements were introduced, notably the wheeled seed-drill which replaced the scattering of seed by hand, and the complementary horse-hoe for weeding between the drills. An essential element in the process of agricultural improvement was enclosure of the open fields and abolition of the strip system of farming, a process which was already well advanced in Chippenham through the consolidation of holdings by a few families. Enclosure usually required an Act of Parliament, and many hundred such acts were passed.

In 1780, Crisp Molyneux, wishing to sell the Chippenham estate, had the leaseholds surveyed and valued. On his valuation, the surveyor noted "An act to be got to enclose (almost the whole Parish being Mr. Montgomerie's) this estate would be amazingly improved. House and offices being covered with lead and very elegantly fitted up, to be valued by two capital surveyors one to be chosen by each side." The Act was approved in 1791, just before Drummond Smith sold the estate to John Tharp of Good Hope, Jamaica in February 1792. The fen, marsh and Latchmere were excluded and the church and cottagers were allotted land in compensation for their small pieces of enclosed land; the total enclosure amounted to 2146 acres. John Tharp wrote on his copy of the Act of Enclosure "obtained by D.S. & was the making of this estate."

Chapter 7

A new dynasty takes over

John Tharp's great-great-grandfather, of the same name (or, perhaps, Thorpe), who is said to have been a Cromwellian general, was one of the earliest English settlers in Jamaica, when it was won from Spain in 1655; the family estates prospered in the following generations. John Tharp, born in 1744, was sent to England for his education at Eton and Trinity College, Cambridge. Back in Jamaica, he married, in 1766, Elizabeth Partridge, co-heir with her brother to the Potosi estate; she died in 1780. He bought the neighbouring Good Hope estate and consolidated a number of sugar plantations run with slave labour around the port of Falmouth. He was also, evidently, something of an entrepreneur. The Tharps had five sons, of whom the second died in infancy, and two daughters. When John Tharp came to England and bought the Chippenham estate, his eldest son Joseph (b. 1766) and next surviving son John (b. 1770) came with him; the younger sons, Thomas and William, stayed in Jamaica.

The eldest son Joseph served in the Life Guards and, in 1788, married Lady Susan Murray, daughter of the Earl of Dunmore. He died, apparently as the result of an accident of some sort, in 1794, leaving a daughter and a son, John, born that same year. He was buried at Chippenham.

When John Tharp bought the Chippenham estate, there were eight enclosed farms, all of which were leasehold on leases of approximately twenty five years. Four of them were over 350 acres, the largest being La Hogue of 640 acres; three were between 95 and 155 acres; and one of 44 acres was farmed by the lessee of the New Goat Inn. In 1797, there were thirteen freehold and copyhold houses and cottages in the village. John Tharpe had bought the rest, having between them forty-five rights of common. The total acreage when John Tharp bought the estate for £40,000 was 2959 acres, and the net rents amounted to about £1550.

The principal common rights had been on the heath land at the south of the village, and the fen area. Some time in the latter half of the 18th century, the heath area had been divided between the three largest farms and brought into cultivation for the first time since the Middle Ages. So, when John Tharp took over, the only common rights which the villagers still held were on the fen (which

31

had already been a cause of dispute in the 16th and 17th centuries). The fen was excluded from the enclosure award, because it was considered to be of little value, but John Tharp thought otherwise. In 1796, he exchanged the common rights of the thirteen cottages which still held them for an allotment of a little over three acres each. He laid down that no cottager was to cut more than three loads of turves (and only under the orders of the reeve), that no cottager was to sell or give away turves, and that no one from outside the parish was to dig them; but he also set aside thirty-six acres for the poor to cut turves for fuel (presumably for the benefit of leaseholders whose rights he had bought with the estate). He then set about to drain, enclose and plant the rest of the fen.

In January 1797, be bought the Badlingham estate for £18,000. This was about 1100 acres and the two estates now comprised about 4100 acres "within a ring fence" and, in the words of John Tharp, "perhaps for the extent, a more complete estate there is not in England". However he had not finished; in October 1798, be bought the Snailwell estate for £27,000. This contained the whole parish, except the glebe land, amounting to about 2500 acres and bringing the whole acreage of John Tharp's estate up to nearly 7000 acres.

At the time of his purchase "The Manor, Mansion House and offices, Garden, Park and Sundry Paddocks enclosed in a brick wall" covered 320 acres. John Tharp enclosed another 30 acres, made a lake fed by springs nearly three-quarters of a mile long, and built large hot-houses. His lasting contribution to the scenery of Chippenham was his plantations, in which he is said to have planted two million trees.

In 1792, he employed seven male servants — two footmen, a coachman, groom, gardener, gamekeeper and a helper in the stables. He had one carriage, five riding horses and two coach horses. By 1800, his establishment had increased to thirteen male servants and he had two four-wheel carriages, two two-wheel carriages, fourteen riding and carriage horses, twenty-three horses for husbandry and sixteen dogs.

He built the north gateway and lodges leading to the High Street; also the eight pairs of semi-detached cottages linked by their washhouses — New Row — between the gateway and the school and, beyond the school, a terrace of four cottages — Maltings Yard. (These cottages have often been mistakenly ascribed to Lord Orford). He planned to extend the Hall; a rough plan, dated 1799, says "it will not have the grandeur of Blenheim, but it will possess what I think of much more importance, which is comfort". The intended architect was James Wyatt, who had already designed the north gateway, but the Hall was not rebuilt as John Tharp, faced with problems on his Jamaican estates, returned there in May 1802.

He left his son John the younger in charge at Chippenham, with a steward running the Home, or Park, Farm. John was an Army officer with no experience of managing a large estate and his father had said that he was to accept guidance from Richard Dashwood of Cley Hall, Norfolk (later one of the executors and

New Row.

trustees of his will). Dashwood and colleagues and the steward appear to have paid little attention to John's wishes and often, it seems, acted in their own interests rather than those of the estate.

Though he had plenty of problems in Jamaica and was in poor health, old John Tharp wrote often to his son concerning the Chippenham estate and particularly his beloved plantations. With regard to finance he wrote "Chippenham barely pays its own way, so that you see what an English estate does and were I to make you a present of it, I should be signing your ruin . . . I am poor indeed in Cambridgeshire".

According to the customary right of primogeniture, the Jamaican and English estates would, on the death of John Tharp, be expected to pass to his grandson - another John, the only son of his deceased eldest son Joseph. This boy (b. 1794) had, since infancy, been described as not behaving like other children. In 1800, his grandfather had put him in the charge of the Rev. Thomas Sisson at Bradfield (Essex). Sisson wrote to John Tharp senior (in Jamaica) that he was very hopeful about young John; that, though he had great difficulty with his pupil's writing, it was improving; that the boy was cheerful, active and very good-tempered. John Tharp wrote to his son in October 1803 "Let me know what you think of John now he has been with you. He is a boy that is affectionate if made much of, but otherwise very shy." If only he had known the true state of his grandson's mind, he might perhaps have ignored primogeniture in his will and saved his son a great deal of trouble.

Only two years after his return to Jamaica, John Tharp died in 1804. His will was long and complex. In an affidavit the following year, one of his trustees wrote that he (Tharp) had "experienced in his lifetime considerable vexation from jealousies and differences arising between the several branches of his family" and had written a will giving fit provision for each, "*to be administered by trustees none of whom were family*". As was to be expected, he left the Jamaican and English estates to his grandson John, then aged ten, and annuities for his children, grandchildren and others to be paid from the revenue of the estates. His son John was to occupy Chippenham Park (paying rents, dues and taxes) and enjoy all the benefits until the grandson attained the age of twenty-four; and the trustees were charged with keeping the estate in good order until that time. They were to plant at least 10,000 trees each year.

Chapter 8

The estate in Chancery

Until his father died, John Tharp (the younger) had simply been looking after the Chippenham estate on his father's behalf — though often frustrated by his father's friends who were supposed to be helping him. Now he was appointed Committee to act for his nephew John during his minority, and the Court of Chancery appointed a Receiver of rents for the Tharp estates in England.

When Clement Tookie died, John Tharp had presented George Laughton D.D. as vicar of Chippenham. He died in 1800 and was buried in the south aisle of the church, where several of his relatives also lie. His granddaughter married Sir Erskine May, Lord Farnborough — the well-known Clerk of the House of Commons -whose marble tomb lies close to the south porch. There is also a memorial window which represents St. Stephen and St. Margaret, recalling both Sir Erskine's connection with the House and the church's own patron saint. The next vicar was Henry Moon, who held the living for only five years.

The trustees of old John Tharp's will then appointed Mr. Sisson as vicar, an action completely contrary to young John Tharp's wishes. Sisson already held two livings and apparently accepted Chippenham with some reluctance, since he had to give up one of these which was a better one. Nevertheless, he did so, young John Tharp was powerless to intervene and Thomas Sisson was vicar of Chippenham for thirty-three years. It was one of the terms of his appointment that he would not live in the village, and he seldom visited his parish. Records show that, during twenty-five years of his incumbency, he performed only six baptisms, one marriage and no funeral. A chaplain came for a service on Sundays. The church fell into disrepair, and suffered from vandalism. Perhaps Mr. Sisson should not be judged too harshly; he was, as will be seen, in a very difficult position vis-à-vis the Tharp family and the trustee/executors. But it is not surprising that it was during his incumbency that, in 1832, a Congregational chapel was built in the village.

The health of his pupil John, the grandson/heir deteriorated; he began to show more evident signs of mental instability and also became subject to epileptic fits. His mother, Lady Susan, had twice remarried after his father's death; her third husband was the Rev. A.E. Douglas, who had a parish in Ireland. In 1813, she wished to remove her son John from Sisson's care and take him to Ireland. This was opposed and he was transferred to the care of another clergyman at Oxford where it was thought that he would get more company than in the Sisson household, and some healthy exercise.

Early in 1815, with John's twenty first birthday approaching, his mother, supported by her family and friends, decided that, before he came of age, he should get married lest "through his inferiority of intellect and imbecility of mind" he should be inveigled into an unsuitable marriage. The trustees of old John Tharp agreed. An engagement was arranged to a Miss Roberts but this was soon revoked in favour of an engagement to Lady Hannah-Charlotte Hay, third daughter of the seventh Marquess of Tweeddale. Eight days after their first introduction to each other, John and Lady Hannah were married in London by John's stepfather, the Rev. Douglas; his uncle John and aunt were not present.

The young couple moved to Scotland, but John reacted disastrously to marriage. There was no love on either side and, from being simple-minded but harmless, John became unmanageable and had, at times, to be physically restrained. In December, his uncle John went north to sort out matters with the family, brought him south and put him into care in London. He was declared insane, and his uncle was appointed Committee to his estate in England subject to supervision by the Master in Lunacy of the Court of Chancery. The following year he was moved to a private asylum at Much Hadham (Herts) kept by a Mr. Jacob, who was widely recognised as a sympathetic and effective guardian of the insane. [In all official documents, this unfortunate man is referred to as "John Tharp, lunatic". I have therefore retained this term, even though it is seldom used now, when mental illnesses are better understood and, to some degree, curable.]

In 1818, when he reached the age of twenty four, the Jamaican and English estates passed to him by his grandfather's will. His wife, Lady Hannah, petitioned that they be allowed to take up residence at Chippenham Park, saying that Mr. Sisson was prepared to move his family to Chippenham and organise a proper establishment for them. There were many good reasons for opposing such a move, and the Court of Chancery ruled against it. John remained at Much Hadham, where he spent most of the rest of his life.

Between the time that old John Tharp returned to Jamaica in 1802 and his death in 1804, a lot of money was spent on Chippenham Park — much of it on unnecessary and shoddy building work — which John Tharp the younger did not approve but could not prevent. After his father's death, when be became Committee for his nephew during his minority, it was the trustees of his father's will and the receiver appointed by the Court who actually received rents and paid for the maintenance of the estate. It was only when he became Committee for his nephew in lunacy that he was able to try to administer the estate to his own satisfaction, though he was subject to the supervision of the Court of Chancery, to which all estate accounts had to be submitted.

Lady Hannah now proposed that Chippenham Park should be let. John Tharp observed that the house was out of character with the park. The park was "so extensive as to be too expensive for a gentleman of moderate income and the house too small for a nobleman or man of large fortune". He described the house as " . . . extremely damp and ill-built and comes more under the denomination of a shooting box than a mansion and, if uninhabited for a season and without good fires, it would go to ruin". In the "best part of the house" there were four moderate sized rooms on the ground floor and four small bedrooms and a very small dressing room on the first floor; offices and attics occupied the wings. Only a member of the family (and he was the heir) could be expected to occupy and maintain the Park; if, however, his nephew ever regained his sanity he would move out at three months notice. So, in 1821, Lady Hannah petitioned that the sum which had been allowed from the estate for upkeep of the Park should be stopped, and that John Tharp should pay rent for occupying it as from 1818, the date on which John the lunatic inherited the estate. The Lord Chancellor, though sympathetic to John Tharp's problems, ruled that this was correct in law. When asked by John's counsel what would happen if he could not afford the rent and the Park proved to be unlettable, the Lord Chancellor replied that, in that case, he would have to allow John Tharp to continue without paying rent since there was no other action by which he could obtain better provision for the lunatic's estate. A rent of £550 per annum was finally agreed.

How did these difficult family problems affect the village? The years following the end of the Napoleonic wars were a time of unrest and protest, much of it arising from the price of corn. A balance between cheap bread for a rising population, a proper income for farmers and decent wages for their labourers was difficult to achieve. The population of the country as a whole doubled between 1801 and 1851, and that of Chippenham rose from 524 to 811.

New leases for the estate farms had been agreed by the receiver in 1812. When John Tharp took over as Committee for his nephew in lunacy, he found the farmhouses in a deplorable state, the cost of necessary repairs being assessed in 1812 at £9,495. The rents of the farms could not, in justice, be retained and they were reduced each year in the early 1820's. When John Tharp granted new leases in 1826, the tenants refused to enter into agreements until the farms were put into repair. All these transactions had to be approved by the Court of Chancery, involving endless petitions, affidavits and legal judgments. John Tharp was careful to say that no blame could be laid on the tenants themselves for the poor state of their properties.

The villagers must have welcomed the light relief provided by the doings of the "fortunate youth" which are told in a small book, dated 1818, with the imposing title "The FORTUNATE YOUTH; or *Chippenham Croesus*: containing the commencement, action, and denouement of the NEWMARKET HOAX, with original observations and various mysterious anecdotes, and midnight adventures connected with LOVE and POLITICS during his two months' extraordinary career; hitherto unpublished." Abraham Cawston, a youth in his late teens, was regarded as a pleasant and intelligent young man, and was said to be courting a lady of fortune. He was the son of a maltster of Chippenham, and his father sent him to a tutor at Shrewsbury to prepare him for the church. During a night stop at Birmingham, en route to Shrewsbury, so his story went, he met an old man who, after many hours of conversation, decided to make him the sole beneficiary of his will. The old man died six weeks later and when Cawston received his papers, he was told that he was now possessed of boundless wealth but that its preservation depended on maintaining a strict secrecy regarding the old man's instructions in the will; his benefactor's objective had been to acquire secret influence, and most foreign sovereigns owed him money.

Cawston employed a respected Newmarket solicitor as his "confidential friend and adviser in the law". He gave instructions for the purchase of various estates, applied for a grant of armorial bearings, and said that half a million pounds would be devoted to his family — on the strength of which his elder brother was entered for Emmanuel College, Cambridge. He received gifts from persons anxious to curry favour, and was wont to leave drafts for large sums of money lying about to be seen by those he wished to impress.

After about two months, a letter was published in the *Morning Post* declaring that Cawston was either a lunatic or an impostor; and every person whom he had named as having had dealings with him denied all knowledge of him. His solicitor, in a signed letter, leapt to his defence declaring that he had complete trust in him -but not for long; two weeks later he wrote another letter admitting that he had been fooled. At the time the bubble burst, the "fortunate youth" was on the continent supposedly visiting his estates; the book unfortunately does not tell what happened to him. It was said that he carried out many small hoaxes in Chippenham and Newmarket; he must, at least, have provided the villagers with plenty of material for gossip.

Though protests involving riotous conduct occurred in various parts of Cambridgeshire, the only open disorder at Chippenham took place in 1830/31. Some paupers of the village started to dig turf and sedge, claiming the ancient right of turbary, on the part of the fen which had been exempted from the Enclosure Act but had been enclosed by old John Tharp. They had a poor legal case, since the right was not a general one but applied only to specific persons (and John Tharp had given compensation to those persons), but they seem to have believed that the lord of the manor would not take the matter to court. The affair came to a head in May 1831 when the paupers started to cut down trees in the plantations and physically threatened the eldest son of the manor and estate staff. The case was taken to court and even those who had some sympathy with the paupers would not countenance violence and withdrew their support.

Mr Sisson was succeeded in 1838, by the Rev. Augustus Tharp, third son of John Tharp the younger who was appointed vicar of Chippenham. In 1854, he became also rector of Snailwell but the two parishes separated again after his death. A new vicarage (now named Longwood) was built to his design in Victorian Gothic style, with elaborate chimneys originally at Landwade Hall.

A singers' gallery was built in the tower arch of the church and an "unpretentious but good" organ installed. The singers were said to have been excellent, and the congregation turned to the west to face them when hymns were sung. The twenty one pieces of church land, amounting to fifteen acres, which had been listed by Clement Tookie, were commuted for one large plot which the vicar let as allotments — a use which has continued to this day.

Augustus Tharp married the daughter of a Suffolk rector, and they had three sons and three daughters. He died in 1877 after nearly forty years as vicar, and was buried in the family vault.

John Tharp had to endure the bureaucracy of the Court of Chancery, perpetual demands from Lady Hannah for money and the unhelpful attitude of his father's executors, for the rest of his life. There were problems too in Jamaica — the estates being, of course, in chancery on behalf of the lunatic, as were the English estates. Lawyers fees for all the litigation involved must have been enormous.

John Tharp's wife Anna Maria seems to have given him great support, and to have taken a major hand in the running of the Park, together with the steward Anthony Holcombe. She died in 1840, and John Tharp himself died in 1851 at the age of eighty one. For nearly fifty years he had done his best to maintain the family estates (of which he was, in fact, himself only a tenant) in the face of the problems arising from his father's will — which he bitterly resented. His father was, he said, the only person who refused to recognise the imbecility of his grandson and to describe him only as being shy, but he and his brother had no opportunity of informing their father of the facts. A marble memorial tablet to John and Anna Maria Tharp was erected by their seven children, to the right of the east window of the church.

The census of 1851 enables us to visualise the village at the time of John Tharp's death, when its population was at its highest ever. There were 150 houses, a population of 811 — 438 males, 373 females; 576 had been born in the village. Eight farmers employed 131 agricultural labourers (of ages ranging from 80 to 11) and five shepherds (one of whom had his thirteen year old daughter as "shepherd's boy"). There were four cordwainers; a blacksmith with two men, an apprentice and a journeyman; a wheelwright with two men and a journeyman; three carpenters and two journeymen; three bricklayer's journeymen. There were two millers, one of whom was a maltster with a carter and journeyman. One of the carpenters was also a brewer. The grocer/draper employed an assistant and a "shopwoman", and his son was a "teacher of pianoforte, organ and English singing". There was also a butcher. The male population could call upon a master tailor, who employed an assistant and two journeymen; while a dressmaker, a sempstress and a strawbonnet maker catered for the women. A shoemaker also had his journeyman, and there were three laundresses. The landlord of the Hope Inn employed a barmaid, an ostler and a bookmaker. The name William Harris, watchmaker, can still be found on grandfather clocks in the village. The schoolmaster and schoolmistress presided over twenty three scholars. And there were thirty two paupers.

A gamekeeper, four grooms and a gardener with four men were presumably employed at the Park. Nine domestic servants at the Park and five at the vicarage were all born outside the village; and Thomas Kent of Badlingham farm, who was a widower of forty, employed a teacher for his five children and four servants none of whom was born in Chippenham. The farmers of La Hogue and Waterhall farms and Joseph Sidney Tharp who was living at The Cottage (the dower house of the estate) also had living-in servants.

The census conveys the impression of a busy, self-sufficient village, but the standard of living of most villagers was no doubt very basic. It is probable that few of the cottages which housed large families had more than two rooms and there were, of course, no "amenities". One of the cottages built by old John Tharp (occupied to-day by a family of three) housed Thomas Bishop, his wife, four sons (one a widower of thirty five) and four grandchildren aged between one and seven; not many were as crowded as this but six or more occupants was common.

With John Tharp at the Hall, his eldest son Joseph at The Cottage and another son Augustus at the vicarage, the Tharps were very obviously predominant in the village; but the census of 1851 records another family dynasty which was to play a leading part in village affairs for the next century and more. The tenants of Badlingham, La Hogue and Waterhall farms were, respectively Thomas (b. 1811), Lewis (b. 1816) and Philip (b. 1814) Kent who were, presumably, brothers and had come from Wilbraham around 1840. By 1871, John Kent (b. 1838) had succeeded his father at Badlingham.

Lewis Kent and his wife Augusta had seven sons and five daughters. Three daughters died in infancy and five sons in their twenties. The eldest son Walter died in 1862, aged twenty, and his funeral was a remarkable occasion considering his youth. Nearly a thousand attended the funeral, next to the hearse was his favourite grey charger, and a volley was fired over the grave by 1st Cambridgeshire Mounted Volunteers, of which he was a member. Lewis Kent himself died in 1876. He had lived in Chippenham for thirty seven years, and was a much respected man in both the village and the neighbourhood; he was a noted hare courser. His second and last surviving son Arthur died at La Hogue in 1881, leaving only his widow and one daughter of this once large family. Augusta Kent died in 1912, aged ninety one. An altar tomb above the family vault in the churchyard, and a window and tablet in the south aisle of the church, commemorate this notable village family.

On the death of John Tharp, his eldest son Joseph Sidney Tharp was appointed Committee for his first cousin, John the lunatic. Joseph Tharp had served in the Coldstream Guards and had, for a time, managed the Jamaican estates. In 1825 he had married Anna Maria Gent who died in 1850, and they had four sons and a daughter. In 1852, he married the Hon. Laura Trollope (b. 1825), daughter of the first Lord Kesteven.

He continued to live at The Cottage (later named the Manor House, and now Chippenham Lodge). The Park was let with shooting rights over the estate and periodical occupation of the Hall (judging from John Tharp's description in 1820 in connection with leasing the estate, the Hall was not a comfortable house). In one of the leases, Joseph Tharp was described as "permissive occupier of the manor lands and shooting". He reserved to himself much of the shooting within the Park wall.

The family was having problems in running the Jamaican estates whose profitability had been falling since the 1830s. In 1864, they were disentailed from old John Tharp's will and sold in 1867.

A national occasion will often spark off a village community; such an occasion was the marriage of the Prince of Wales (later Edward VII) early in 1863. "Early in the morning the bells rang merrily, and the village presented a scene of gaiety such as was never before seen at Chippenham". The chief organiser was the curate. There were flags everywhere and "gigantic arches", made by the schoolmaster, spanned the main street. A church service (with litany and sermon) was held at 1 p.m. Then, in "booths" in the vicarage garden, after a sung grace, all the poor of the village over sixty years of age sat down to a meal of beef, plum pudding and ale, each employer presiding over his own men and their wives. After dinner, the villagers, preceded by a band, marched to the sports field; activities continued till dark, when the vicar and schoolmaster gave a firework display. The celebrations finished at 9 p.m. when Lewis Kent called for three cheers each for the families of the squire, vicar and curate.

Agriculture prospered in the middle years of the 19th century but, while they were good times for landlords and farmers, agricultural labourers received little benefit. So, when the government, in 1871, recognised a limited right to form trades unions, "agricultural welfare societies" came into being. The South Cambridgeshire Agricultural Labourers Society, the first union to be formed in the county, had some initial success, but not for long. In 1874, a Newmarket Farmers' Defence Association declared a lock-out of union members and a maximum wage of 13s. per week. This is commemorated in Chippenham by the "Union tree", a horse chestnut, planted at the fork at the north end of the High Street on the site where the agricultural workers held their meetings. (The tree is dying, probably as a result of nearby road works, and is to be replaced). The last years of the century saw the collapse of English agriculture as it had been practised for centuries. Free trade allowed the import of corn from the vast prairies of America, less land was devoted to wheat and more to pasture or other uses. Many farm labourers migrated to the towns or abroad. In Chippenham, the population dropped from 722 in 1871 to 612 in 1891.

In 1873, Joseph Tharp gave £500 towards supplying coal annually to the

Scotland End and Union tree, 1906.

deserving poor of Chippenham and Snailwell. He died in 1875, and his wife died in 1877. His eldest son died only six weeks after him, his second son had died in 1873 and his fourth son in infancy, so the estate passed to his third and only surviving son, William Montagu Tharp.

The east end of the south aisle became a Tharp memorial chapel, above a family vault with access from outside the church. Joseph Tharp, his wife Laura, his three sons, and the Rev. Augustus Tharp are interred there. The east window of the chapel was given by Montagu Tharp in memory of his brothers and sister, and the south window in memory of Augustus Tharp by his widow.

Chapter 9

The English country house

As a young man, William Montagu Gent-Tharp (b. 1837) had served in the Crimean war as a captain in the 62nd regiment. In 1861, he hyphenated his name with Gent in accordance with the will of his maternal uncle and godfather, George Gent of Moyns Park Essex, and was the principal beneficiary of his estate. He married, in 1868, Annabella Lucy Annesley who was a sister-in-law of his second cousin, Horace Neville Tharp.

When Montagu succeeded his father, he took up residence at the Hall, and had a survey of the estate made; this was recorded in a superb volume of maps, with the tenants of all the estate properties — farms and cott-ages — named. Old John Tharp's Chippenham estate was still intact. A rental of 1881 shows that all the farms were leased, mostly on one-year tenancies at about £1 per acre; Park, or Hall, farm was round the Park; Church farm round the back of the church and glebeland; Badlingham to the

"Monty" Tharp.

43

east; La Hogue, Waterhall and Grange to the south; and two farms without their own farmhouses and referred to only by their tenants' names to the north. Small pieces of land, mostly near the fen, were leased to villagers. There were two large farms at Snailwell. At that time, the present High Street was, from the Park gates to the pump, known as Park Street with New Row and Maltings Yard on the west side; Village Street ran from the pump northwards with Rodney Square and Palace Yard on the west side and Queen Square and Sidney Row on the east side; the north end of Village Street was known as Scotland End.

Lady Hannah Tharp died in 1876, and John the lunatic at Much Hadham early in 1883 at the age of 89. "Monty" Tharp now enjoyed complete ownership of the Chippenham Park estate. In July, he laid on a great firework display by James Paine to celebrate his accession. The final set-piece was a "Fire Portrait" of him ("correct likeness guaranteed") with the motto "Prosperity to Chippenham and Snailwell". He then set about rebuilding the Hall in a Queen Anne Revival style, incorporating parts of the older houses and greatly increasing its size. The years from the 1870s to the outbreak of war in 1914 have been described as the golden age of the English country house. Hospitality on a large scale was a feature of such houses, and it is a reflection of the times that Monty Tharp should have built such a large house although he had no children. A newspaper called it "a pleasure house of lordly dimensions".

Racing at Newmarket attracted many of the aristocracy and this provided an incentive for the development of organised shooting on estates in the area. Chippenham was for many years one of the leading shooting properties; indeed, it laid claim to have been the birthplace of partridge-driving. The partridge was at that time the principal game bird, though pheasants were also reared; hares were plentiful and were shot in great numbers. During the 20th century, changes in farming methods and loss of hedgerows have deprived partridges of their natural food and winter cover and they have become comparatively scarce. The Prince of Wales (later King Edward VII) — with the Marquess of Londonderry, Earl Cadogan and six other guns — took part in partridge drives at Chippenham in October 1887 and 1893; and in 1896, he and the Duke of Cambridge stayed at the Park for shooting. There is a picture of the old Hall with the date 1886, probably painted shortly before rebuilding started. This took several years and is believed to have been completed about 1895 — a fit mansion in which to entertain the heir to the throne. While on the subject of shooting, it is worth mentioning that, early in the century, John Tharp had complained that it cost about £300 a year to maintain a herd of deer in the park; heavy shot has been found in trees felled this century.

The chancel of the church was restored and a new chancel arch built in 1885, and an east window was inserted in memory of Joseph Sidney Tharp and his second wife, Laura. In 1893, the nave was restored, the gallery at the west end removed and a new font installed. The piers on the N. side are alternately circular and octagonal; those on the S. side were replaced by "a curiously bleak

1893 shooting party. Edward, Prince of Wales centre, Monty Tharp second from left.

design". (N. Pevsner). Seven hatchments have recently been restored and hung in the clerestory; they bear the arms of Lord Orford, George Montgomerie and his wife, and four members of the Tharp family. In 1898, three bells were recast and rehung, and a sixth bell was given by Mr. de la Rue, the occupant of The Cottage.

In December 1894, the first meeting of the Parish Council, formed under the Local Government Act, was held. As a result, letters were written to the lord of the manor complaining of overcrowding in the village, even though the population had fallen steadily since 1851 to a figure of 612 in 1891. At the same time, the Newmarket Sanitary Authority wrote to Mr Tharp's agent and to the vicar calling attention to the fact that, in the cottage occupied by Alfred Moss, there were thirteen persons sleeping in three very small bedrooms. They said that Mr. Tharp had provided a new earth closet which was a great improvement, but suggested that he should be asked to give Mr. Moss notice to quit. Only a terrace of four small cottages and a larger semi-detached pair bear plaques reading WMT 1880 and WMT 1899 respectively, so it does not seem that he did much to increase the housing stock in the village.

In 1890, the Hope Inn was renamed Tharp Arms. In the same year, 650 acres of heath land adjoining the Newmarket-Bury St. Edmunds road, known as Lime Kilns, was leased to the Jockey Club for twenty eight years. This was later sold to them, and is one of the principal training grounds for Newmarket racehorses.

In that year also, a notable villager, Anthony Holcombe, died at the age of ninety eight. He had been steward of the estate in the difficult days of the 1820s, and was a trusted servant of the Tharps all his life. He used to say "Mr. Tharp says he'll keep me till I'm a hundred — and then he'll shoot me". He was a great-great-grandfather; a very unusual record. Another villager with a remarkable family record was Arthur Drake, who died in 1914 at the age of eighty eight. He was a saddler in the village for over fifty years. Forty two of his children and grandchildren were present at his funeral, and the total number of his descendants living at that time was seventy.

On a Saturday night in February 1899, a fire started at a small farm in the centre of the village. There was no water supply except the common well and, before help could be obtained from outside, much of the centre of the village was destroyed. The school was opened to the homeless, some found accommodation with friends, but others left the village altogether. The population fell from 612 in 1891 to only 500 in 1901.

Montague Tharp was a JP and a Deputy Lieutenant for Cambridgeshire. He died in 1899. In his will he wrote "It is my earnest wish that my said dear wife and cousin successively will continue the management of the estate and maintain and improve it the same as in my lifetime".

The cousin mentioned in Montagu Tharp's will was Arthur Keane Tharp (b. 1848) second son of Rev. Augustus Tharp. He was the heir to the entailed estate, subject to the life tenancy of Monty's widow Annabella. Arthur Tharp was a

1906. T. W. Sier, Postmaster, Grocer and Draper.

widower and did not live at Chippenham. In 1908, he proposed that the estate should be sold, arguing that investment of the proceeds would provide a better income than the rentals of the farms. That, of course, would depend on what price was obtained. Arthur maintained that, with the current interest in Newmarket of the king and members of the aristocracy, there would never be a better time to sell; others thought the suggested valuations were wildly optimistic. Arthur wrote to Annabella that "sooner or later the property must go out of the family, as it is conspicuously the luxury of the rich", but she would not countenance the sale.

She enjoyed life in high society, not only at Chippenham but in London and Italy, where the family owned a villa. The shooting was, for some years let to Sir Ernest Cassel, the financier, philanthropist and friend of Edward VII. The king shot at Chippenham in October 1904 and three times in October 1906, and the Prince of Wales (later King George V) shot in 1907 and again, when king, in 1912.

Relations between Annabella and Arthur evidently deteriorated and, in 1916, they resorted to litigation to settle the succession. Monty Tharp had left the estate to Arthur and then "in tail male"; if this line failed it was to pass to his second cousin, Horace Neville Tharp and his successors in tail male. Arthur was a widower with no sons. Neville had married Annabella's sister Augusta and had two sons; he had died in 1902. Annabella, naturally, supported the claim of the eldest son, her nephew Gerard. A settlement was reached under which the estate

47

New Street, 1913.

was disentailed and Gerard would succeed on Annabella's death; Arthur would receive an agreed sum of money from the estate.

Members of the Kent family were prominent in the village community for the whole of the first half of this century. At this time Harold Arthur Kent (1878-1943), a grandson of Lewis Kent, was tenant of La Hogue farm, and John Kent was still at Badlingham (They were distant cousins). John Kent died in 1927 at the age of ninety and, about this time Harold Kent became tenant of Badlingham. He had already quitted La Hogue Hall, though continuing to run the farm, because the dampness of the house was affecting his health, (the deaths of Lewis Kent's young family were chiefly due to tuberculosis).

Parish records contain little information about the village during the 1914-18 war. The Hall was not used as a convalescent home for wounded soldiers, as were many large houses during the war. Agriculture was, of course, vital to the country but, after conscription had been introduced early in 1916, agricultural workers were not automatically exempted from service; employers had to apply through a tribunal. When Harold Kent of La Hogue farm applied for exemption for three of his labourers in October 1916, he told the Newmarket Rural Tribunal that he was trying to form a Chippenham Volunteer Force, and had a wounded soldier who would drill them. These Volunteer Forces (the equivalent of the WW2 Home Guard) were formed in almost all villages, and it became a condition of exemption for an agricultural worker that he should join the Volunteers. Training and drills, outside their working hours, were coordinated on a county basis.

Coronation Cottages (built 1911).

A typical claim for exemption was made by the tenant of Church Farm on behalf of his horsekeeper, aged thirty two. He told the tribunal that he farmed 250 acres of which 40 were grass; he had 7 horses, 15 cows and one bull, 13 store beasts, 20 pigs and 80 sheep; he employed five men and two boys. This type of farming soon disappeared with the introduction of machinery and chemical fertilisers. The main crops are now wheat, barley and sugar-beet. Removal of hedges to facilitate the use of the combine harvester has created a landscape resembling, to some degree, the open fields before enclosure.

Twenty one villagers were killed in action during the war.

Annabella Tharp was nearly eighty years of age when the war ended. Taxation had weighed heavily on the finances of the estate, but it was still the chief source of employment for villagers. The shooting was let; in 1921, Mrs. Tharp wrote "Very few hares, having been shot by *everyone*!! during the war years". Although Mrs. Tharp and a niece were the only permanent residents of the Hall, the octogenarian lady of the manor still enjoyed the social way of life, and employed a domestic staff of about fifteen. In 1922, the Princess Royal and her husband Lord Lascelles stayed at the Hall; and every October a large house party was assembled for Newmarket races. The west wing of the house was the servants' wing, and most of the guest bedrooms were in the east wing. About twenty bedrooms had fireplaces to which coal had to be transported — water too, for there were no bathrooms in the wing.

The population of the village was very steady at around 500 for the first twenty

49

years of the century, but dropped from 481 in 1921 to 394 in 1931. This was evidently due partly to shortage of housing. Although the Housing Act of 1919 paved the way for the provision of council houses, no houses were in fact built in Chippenham by the local authority until after the second world war. In December 1923, the parish council asked that where a large estate cottage was occupied by only one person, the occupier should be moved to a smaller one; and, in 1926, the parish council and the district council remarked on the difficulty of acquiring building land in the village although they were both in favour of new building "to improve the status of the village". Presumably, the estate could not afford to build new housing, but did not wish to sell land.

The growth of motor traffic began to be felt in the 1920s. In 1922, the parish council asked the district council that "the roads leading from the village to the main roads should be kept in better order and more suitable for motor traffic"; and in 1928, they asked for some improvement to be made at the entrance of New Street as, owing to the development of motor traffic, the spot had become dangerous to the public (it still is).

Chapter 10

A changing village

Arthur Tharp died in 1928 [a year before Annabella] and was interred in the family vault. Villagers were admitted to the vault after the funeral, as had been the custom. This was the last burial there, the vault was sealed and the entrance filled in. When Annabella died the estate passed to the cadet branch of the family, descended from old John Tharp's fourth son, the new lord of the manor being Gerard Tharp [b. 1870]. He was a lieutenant colonel in the Rifle Brigade and had served in the South African and 1914-18 wars. He married, in 1918, Dora Maryan Morris, whose husband had been killed early in the war. They had a son who, in 1927, became the third Baron Killanin. The Tharps had a daughter, Philippa [b. 1918], who was an invalid all her life, and a son, John [b. 1922]. They had been living at The Cottage which had been re-named the Manor House.

In 1929 a carpenter's workshop was converted and equipped as a village hall; a bowling green was laid in the yard. In the late 1930s bowlers moved to a former tennis court within the park, where the first pavilion was erected in 1964; but new greens were laid at the present site in 1967-69 and a new pavilion in 1980 heralded the flourishing Bowls Club of today.

In 1933 the parish council requested the district council to tar New Street as "considerable trouble was experienced with dust by the residents."

Gerard Tharp was responsible for the formation of a branch of the British Legion in Chippenham and Snailwell. Its standard was dedicated in May 1934, shortly after his death, with a parade in the park at which Field Marshal Sir William [later Lord] Birdwood took the salute. The march past was led by the Newmarket town band, seven contingents from neighbouring towns and villages and the scouts from Chippenham and Snailwell were also on parade. Lord Killanin became president. The branch, though now small, is still active; there have been only three standard bearers in the sixty years.

Gerard Tharp died in March 1934, and his widow took over the estate during the minority of the heir, John. Gerard and Dora Tharp had, in 1932, registered the estate as the Chippenham Park Estate Company.

Hospitality at the Park was no longer dispensed on the scale of earlier days, but the estate was, directly or indirectly, responsible for the employment of most of the villagers either in the park itself or on the farms. The estate employed its own labour force, which did all the maintenance work on the farms and properties. Shortly before the war there were about two dozen estate workers and seven gardeners.

The pride of the garden was Lord Orford's walled kitchen garden. In summer it had the appearance of a brilliantly coloured flower garden, but behind the flower borders along the paths were all manner of vegetables and fruit. A pear tree on one of the walls carried five different varieties of pear, and gooseberries were grown on pyramidal bushes five feet high or more. Extensive lawns surrounded the Hall and there was little in the way of garden machinery, so the gardeners were kept busy six days a week. An advertisement for the shooting in 1935 stated: "very good stock of partridges left."

There was still no piped water supply to the village. The New Row cottages had individual pumps for every four houses, and the Maltings Yard had a well, but the only source of water for most villagers was the pump at the centre of the village. In 1934, the parish council said that, although supply had been adequate that year, they would wish to be included in any scheme for a district supply, but were not particularly interested in a sewage disposal scheme. The following year they asked the district council to consider providing an artesian well at the south end of the village; when the district council replied that they would do so but that the cost would be charged on the parish, the matter was dropped. In 1936, the provision of street lighting was discussed with the local electricity company, but the villagers decided against it at a parish meeting, again on the grounds of cost.

In 1937, two seats were placed in the village to commemorate the coronation of King George VI and Queen Elizabeth, and school children planted lime trees in front of the school (alternate trees were removed in 1948 and a pollarding routine was instituted). Then came the war. A Parish Home Food Production Committee was formed (as part of a county effort) "to see that the village is self-supporting and every garden and piece of land cultivated for food". That was the end of the Park's walled garden.

When the vicar (Rev. E.W. Deacon) died in 1942, the vicarage built by Rev. Augustus Tharp was sold and the rector of Snailwell (Rev. J. Purdue) was appointed to Chippenham. The parishes have continued in plurality since then, and the parish of Isleham was added to the vicar of Chippenham's incumbency in 1976. A new vicarage was built at the corner of High Street and New Street in 1974.

During the war, until 1944, there were three military camps in the park; two had NAAFIs and one a YMCA, which were staffed by women of the village. Beetroot and onion sandwiches were very popular! Tanks were a familiar sight in the village; one demolished a house opposite the pump. Both King George VI and General Montgomery visited the troops during run-up to D-day in 1944. In the early days of the war, about forty expectant mothers were housed in the east wing of the Hall, but they did not enjoy the country and moved back to town as soon as they could. The west wing was let as a hospital. A school from Hoxton, north London, was evacuated to Chippenham and Wicken. Mr. Cooper, their schoolmaster, came with the Chippenham contingent, and relations between town and country seem to have been very satisfactory. In June 1943, there were 39 local and 33 evacuee children at the school. For some time at the end of the war, there was a camp for Polish refugees in the park.

Five villagers were killed on active service, including John Tharp, the heir to the estate, and Patrick Hely-Hutchinson, son of the owners of the Manor House.

There had been a Working Men's Club and Reading Room in the village. After the war, this was taken over as a British Legion Club — a move which created some ill-feeling, since many of the villagers had been in "reserved occupations" as agricultural workers and were only allowed to join the club as honorary members.

In 1945, one of the well-known red telephone kiosks was placed in the village and now enjoys almost "listed" status.

In 1947, Dora Tharp handed over the village hall and the land on which it stood to the parish. Early in 1948, nine pairs of "Airy" houses — the first public housing in the village — were built at the top of New Street and named Tharp Way; six old cottages at Scotland End were demolished. Mrs. Tharp and Mrs. Hely-Hutchinson also each built a pair of houses in memory of their sons. Mrs. Tharp's pair remains at the disposal of the estate. The other pair was handed over to the district council with the hope expressed that the houses would be let to Chippenham ex-service men employed in agriculture; they were sold to the parish council for £1 each in 1972.

The laying of water mains was started, standpipes being provided at intervals in the High Street and New Street until such time as pipes could be run from the mains to the properties and drainage be provided at the cottages. New cesspits were dug, but it was not until the late 1960s that a main sewer was laid. An agreement for street lighting was signed in 1946, but this was not actually provided (four lights in the High Street, two in New Street) until 1950; additional lights were provided in later years.

Dora Tharp died in July 1948; she had been a magistrate and County Councillor and was the County Controller of the Women's Volunteer Service (WVS) during the war. The entry for "Tharp of Chippenham Park" now disappeared from the pages of Burke's Landed Gentry. The owner of the estate had always been recorded in it as the "lord of the manor", though it is more likely that John Tharp and his successors had been known as the "squire".

The old chapel of the Knights Hospitallers in the church was restored, and rededicated as a Tharp Memorial chapel by the Bishop of Ely in October 1948; and it was decided to build a bus shelter as a War Memorial, for which donations were invited.

The estate now had to sell a lot of land to meet death duties. The northern fields which had been named Manor Farm, together with Church, Badlingham and La Hogue Farms were all sold to Walter Simpson in 1949. He was a widower aged 73 whose wife, older than himself, had died five years earlier. They had six sons and a daughter. Walter Simpson had made his money mainly by modest but shrewd trading in livestock; he believed in short-term profits and saving. He had worked the mill on the Isleham road, but now lived in the 17th and 19th century farmhouses (36/37 High Street) which had been converted to a single house. He sold Church Farm to his solicitor but bought it back three years later. He sold Badlingham to Arthur Kent (1910-74) who had succeeded his father Harold as a tenant; a new farmhouse had been built in 1936. He sold La Hogue to Richard Tilbrook, who had been tenant since 1944. When he died in 1956, he left Church Farm to his eldest son Oliver, who built a new house and let the old farmhouse. He left Manor Farm to his second son Henry, who was a bachelor; his sister lived with him, later built a new house, and took over the farm after his death in 1980.

Chapter 11

The post-war village

On the death of Mrs. Dora Tharp, the estate passed to Basil Bacon (b. 1904), the son of Gerard Tharp's sister Beatrix. He had been with the Hong Kong and Shanghai Bank for twenty years, and was a prisoner-of-war for three and a half years after the fall of Singapore. After the war he and his wife and daughter came to Chippenham and lived at Church Farmhouse; when he inherited the estate, the family moved to the Hall. The era of large domestic staffs had passed; the wings of the house were let though it was some time before the west wing, which had been the servants' quarters, was modernised. Though, as a member of the family, Mr. Bacon had stayed at Chippenham in earlier days, he had not expected to succeed to the estate and was not well known to the villagers; but he soon played an active part in all village activities. His principal interest lay in the care of the woodlands, and it is estimated that about 750,000 trees were planted during his ownership of the estate. The wood-yard was a busy place, with home-grown timber being used for all maintenance work on the estate. He used to walk the whole estate every week.

The shooting was let to syndicates. While, for some years, hares were plentiful and the annual bag of pheasants was over 2000, that of partridges was barely 100. By the 1980s, partridges had become very scarce and very few hares were shot.

The bus shelter was opened by Lord Killanin, and dedicated as a war memorial, in January 1949. The population of the village in 1951 was 437. A start was made on modernising the New Row cottages, three pairs being done by estate labour. In 1950 a 30 mph speed limit was imposed in the High Street; and in 1952, the streets were given their present official names — High Street, New Street, Palace Lane, Tharp Way and La Hogue Road. In 1955, the village hall was described as very dilapidated, not worth redecorating and too small; the parish council agreed "that the village hall committee should proceed with the possible building of a new hall". Such a task was obviously quite beyond them, and the hall lasted a further thirty eight years.

Basil Bacon served on the district council and held several posts on school boards in East Cambridgeshire. He died rather suddenly (in one of his woodlands) on Christmas Eve 1958, having been in poor health for about five years as a result of his wartime imprisonment. He was greatly esteemed in Chippenham and Snailwell. Life interest in the estate passed to his widow Dorothy.

In 1960, Badlingham farm was divided. Part, including the farmhouse, retained the name and was sold to Lionel Broad. Guy Kent, son of Arthur, farmed the other part under the name of Blandings Farm. He sold this in 1988.

The village pump.

The population had dropped to 366 in 1961, but did not alter much during the next decade, being 352 in 1971. The appearance of the village was attractive and, in 1960, Chippenham won the Best Kept Village competition for Cambridge-shire, founded by Lord Fairhaven of Anglesey Abbey. Half the prize money of £50 was used to lay on water to the churchyard. The village was restricted from entry the next two years but won again in 1963, came second in 1966 and first again in 1967. The parish council, dissatisfied with the appearance of the village, did not enter the competition again until 1971, when they decided to do so in an endeavour to persuade people to keep the village tidy. The unflattering report of the judges was "No great effort made in Chippenham". This was a sign of the times, and parish council minutes often express despondency about life in the village through the 1970s. Villagers recall a constant refrain by the vicar at this time — "the village is dying". When this vicar resigned in 1972, he told the local newspaper that he found the villagers uncooperative and feudal in their outlook and expected their priest to take care of the churches but not to preach sermons. The fundamental problems were lack of jobs, shortage of housing and a consequent further drop in population to 310 in 1981 — the lowest figure since censuses were started in 1801 and probably the smallest for about 400 years.

Money for public housing was short. In 1975, plans were agreed for a mixture of houses to let and plots for sale at the back of Tharp Way, but nothing was built though two semi-detached houses were built on New Street. At a meeting in 1977, district council officers told the parish council that their allocation of money was exhausted, that very few names from the village were on their housing list, and that Chippenham did not feature in the current building programme. However in 1979, the district council built eight small "starter homes" for sale at the end of Tharp Way. In the same year they asked the estate to improve their properties and to sell some of their vacant land for private development. The parish council commented that, while they would like to see the New Row houses modernised, there were problems in the rehousing of tenants.

These unmodernised cottages in New Row and Maltings Yard were becoming very dilapidated. In 1975, the estate had said that water could not be laid on while a current rent freeze was in force, but that it was hoped to provide standpipes to houses without water supply; if tenants would help towards the cost, water could be laid on to the houses.

The Queen's Silver Jubilee in 1977 brought some much needed life to the village. A committee was formed in October 1976 and fund raising events were held at intervals throughout the winter. Snailwell village was invited to join in. Mugs were bought for all school children. On 7 June 1977, celebrations were held in the barn and a marquee at the Park — a fancy dress parade for children, sports and tea in the afternoon; a dance and fancy dress parade for adults in the evening. About 350 people attended and over £700 was raised; half of this was spent on the catering, and the balance divided between the two villages. Chippenham's share was used to provide a notice board for the church, and contributions were made to the national appeal and to village hall funds. Encouraged by the success of this endeavour, a community group was formed "to prevent village life stagnating".

The village received another blow when the school closed in 1978. Although it was recognised that this was inevitable and the children were transferred to the preferred choice of school at Isleham, it was nevertheless a sad event after a history of two hundred and seventy years. The School House was offered to the parish council for a village hall at a very reasonable figure but it was decided, inevitably, that the village could not afford to buy and maintain such a building. {The history of the school is in Appendix 1]

During the early 1980s, two pairs of the New Row cottages were restored and converted to single dwellings, the small terrace built at the same time (Maltings Yard) was demolished and rebuilt as a single house (the original style of its roof line and dormer windows being retained), and the school was converted to a private house (the appearance of its original facade being restored by the demolition of an extension which no present day planner would have allowed). Mrs. Bacon died in 1985, much to the sorrow of the villagers, and was succeeded by her daughter Mrs. Anne Crawley. In that year, the parish council agreed on a partnership scheme with the district council for building twenty-one houses for sale on land owned by the parish behind Tharp Way. This was put out to tender in March 1986 and completed in October 1987; in the event, only one of these houses was occupied by a member of an old village family. Lord Orford's stable block in the Park was converted to houses and flats, and its clock tower renewed.

During the 1980s, other houses were built or converted from uninhabited buildings, as newcomers moved into the village, amounting to about fifty new dwellings including a block of four flats built by the local authority on New Street. At the 1991 census there was a population of 394 in 175 households, compared with 310 in 122 households in 1981.

Chapter 12

The village to-day

Manor Farm was sold piecemeal in the 1980s, and this caused a great change. The barns were converted to houses, and much of the northern fields of the village is now occupied by two studs, a horse-transport business and a deer farm. Horses have become a familiar feature of the village following the setting up of a riding school at the former Longwood stables.

Though the village is surrounded by farmland, it is no longer an agricultural community. The change in the nature of the population in a single decade is shown very clearly by the fact that in 1991, ninety-one houses were owner-occupied compared with thirty-two in 1981. Almost all the new residents who are in employment work in neighbouring towns; in 1991, 44% of households owned more than one car. However, the increase in population has not been enough to support the village shops, the last two of which have closed, while the post office is open only two mornings a week.

In 1987, the Chippenham Park Estate tabled a plan for development of land behind the village hall, but this was withdrawn following criticism that it was too large and out of keeping with the village. A new plan for twenty four houses of more modest size was welcomed by residents at a parish meeting, and received outline planning approval; but, owing to recession in the housing market, it has not yet been started. A spin-off from this plan was that the estate would build a new village hall, while the village would pay for the fittings.

The appearance of the village has improved considerably. The new village hall has been built; a village sign (carved by the owner of the deer farm) has been erected; the former bakery (the oldest house in the village), which had been allowed to fall into such disrepair that it was an eyesore in the centre of the village, is being restored with its facade decorated with pargeting; the old Church Farmhouse has been restored, and its stables are to be taken in hand; the old Church Farm barns are being converted to houses. It is to be hoped that the three outstanding New Row cottages will be modernised before long. The village will then be a place of which the residents can be proud.

When the development behind the village hall and other lesser developments

59

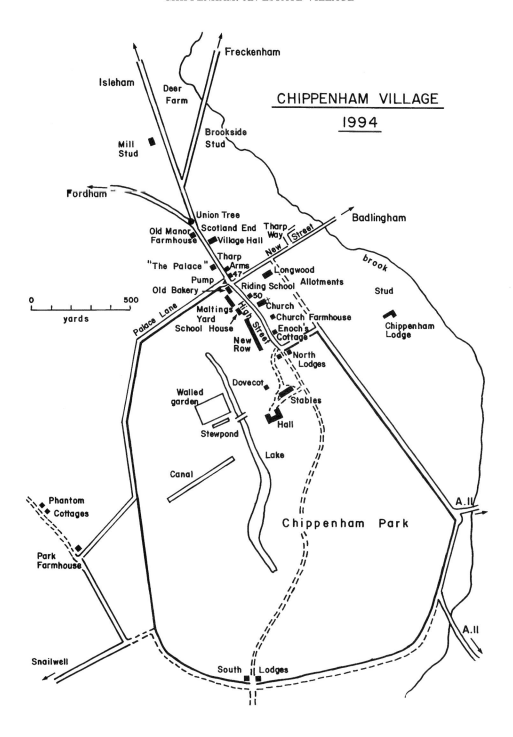

CHIPPENHAM VILLAGE
1994

Freckenham

Isleham

Deer
Farm

Mill
Stud

Brookside
Stud

Fordham

Union Tree

Scotland End
Old Manor
Farmhouse

Tharp
Way

Village Hall

New Street

Badlingham

Tharp
Arms

"The Palace"

47

Pump

Old Bakery

Riding School

50

Church

Longwood

Allotments

brook

Stud

Maltings
Yard

School House

New
Row

Church Farmhouse

Enoch's
Cottage

Chippenham
Lodge

Palace Lane

High Street

North
Lodges

0   500

yards

Walled
garden

Dovecot

Stewpond

Hall

Stables

Canal

Lake

A.11

Phantom
Cottages

Chippenham   Park

Park
Farmhouse

A.11

Snailwell

South   Lodges

The oldest house in the village, formerly the bakery.

have been completed, the population may be expected to rise to between 450 and 500. This should be a large enough community to maintain a lively village, though it is unlikely to be high enough to sustain a shop. Meanwhile, in 1993, Chippenham won the competition for the best kept village in East Cambridgeshire, twenty six years after its last success.

The arrival of newcomers has, also, gradually brought more life to the village. A Youth Club has been revived; a Playscheme group has raised substantial funds and, with the aid of a generous grant from the district council, has equipped a play area to a very high standard; football and cricket teams have been formed, and (again with a grant from the district council) a splendid cricket field has been created on grounds within the park; a Garden Society, with a good membership, provides evening meetings during the winter months and two shows in the summer; extensive repairs have been carried out to the 15th century tower of the church, and fund-raising events are being held in order to repay a loan over a four year period.

Though the Chippenham Park Estate still owns properties in the village and a considerable area of farm land in the parish, the village is no longer dependent on the "lord of the manor" as it was for centuries; it continues, nevertheless, to enjoy the benefits of an estate village. The estate provided the new village hall, and both the bowls club and cricket ground are within the park. Villagers have access to the park, and it provides a perfect setting for shows and fund-raising events.

The gardens have been opened for Daffodil Sunday each spring for many years. The present owners have opened up neglected parts of the gardens, and have made extensive plantings of trees and shrubs. The gardens are now opened for charities several times a year.

The 20th century has seen changes in the life of the village as great, perhaps, as any that have gone before. It remains, nevertheless, a small compact village, recognisably the same as in past centuries; free, so far at least, of the type of housing estate which has spoilt so many villages, and with a population shaping a community life relative to the circumstances of the present day. In the words of Monty Tharp's fireworks display, let us wish "Prosperity to Chippenham" — and, of course, to Snailwell too.

The new village hall.

Appendix 1
The village charities

Lord Orford's Endowed School

The school house was built on the site of the Knights' preceptory towards the end of the 17th century, and was converted and endowed by Lord Orford in 1708. The facade was altered in the 19th century, when the original triangular pediment was removed. the terracotta urns on the parapet were added about 1930. The north west end of the building was the headmaster's house, on two storeys. The rest of the building was a large classroom of one storey. Between the back of the house and the entrance to the cellars an extension was built in the 19th century, and used to cook and dispense soup to the needy of the village; this was converted to a staff room in 1968.

Lord Orford, in his will, left £20 to be paid out of the estate annually to pay the schoolmaster. He intended that all the children of the village should attend. By 1730, the school was associated with the Society for Promoting Christian Knowledge, but in that year there were only six boy and six girl pupils. For many years thereafter, children did not stay at school for more than two or three years and were frequently absent between springtime and harvest, helping in the fields; the number of pupils varied greatly over the years.

In 1837, the Charity Commission gave the school a very complimentary report:- "The annuity of £20 is paid to a schoolmaster, appointed by the Lord of the Manor, by whom 40 boys and girls from 8 to 14 are instructed in reading, writing and arithmetic. Two or three pay scholars from adjoining parishes are included in this number . . . scholars are in regular attendance unless when employed in field labour . . . There is an evening school from six to eight for which a penny a night is charged by the master . . . From 15 to 20 girls whose ages vary from 10 to 12, and boys and young men, whose ages vary from 15 to 20, attend with great regularity and make greater progress than at day school. The revenues of the school are not sufficient to remunerate the master, who could not maintain it but for his private income. It appears to be very well conducted. There are three dame schools in the village, where children are instructed in sewing and spelling." The 1851 census records twenty-one "scholars", and in 1876 there were 76 children at the school. In 1901, there were 67 in the "mixed" school and 42 in the infants' school.

In 1935, responsibility for the school was transferred to the county council, and

Lord Orford's Endowed School, 1914.

six managers were appointed of whom two were from the parish council. During the war, school attendance was boosted by the addition of evacuee children and there were 72 pupils in 1943.

In 1954, the school was reorganised as a primary school for infants and juniors, and seniors went first to Burwell secondary school and then, in 1958, to Soham village college; there were 51 children left in the school. In 1977, the twelve infants then at the school were transferred to Isleham, leaving fourteen juniors at Chippenham. These went to Isleham a few months later and in July 1978 the school was closed, after two hundred and seventy years at the centre of village life. A service of farewell was followed by a reception for a hundred and seventy. There had been many teachers during those years, but none more universally loved and respected than Miss K. Bridgeman, who was headmistress from 1929 to 1959.

The annuity of £20, originally the schoolmaster's salary, was redeemed by the estate in 1949 and the capital invested. For some years the income was used to pay for transport for annual school outings.

The Town Money

At their first meeting in 1894, the parish council assumed responsibility for village charities:-

Lord Orford's Charity — an annuity of £10 left by him in 1727 "for poor householders not in receipt of parish relief".

The School House, from the Church tower.

Tetsal's Charity — early in the 18th century, an unknown donor left £60 in the hands of John Tetsal to be invested; the annual dividend in 1894 was £2.10s.

These two charities were charges on the Chippenham Park estate.

Sir Thomas Revett's Charity — the dividend from Revett's bequest of 1582 was, in 1894, £4.4s.8d. This was payable by the Worshipful Company of Mercers.

The Poor's Land — in 1679, Thomas Delamore left 16¾ acres of the open fields for the benefit of the poor of the village. After the fields were enclosed at the end of the 18th century, 10 acres of land were declared tithe-free in place of the 16¾ acres which were subject to tithe. This was only belatedly discovered, in an early document, when the land was measured in 1952 and found to be only 10 acres.

All this was known as the Town Money and was divided among agricultural labourers, their wives and children under the age of fourteen, widows and widowers, in equal shares. In 1900, 240 recipients received 1s.10d per head, and for many years thereafter the average sum was about 2s.

In January 1933, at a time of serious unemployment, the rental of the Poor's Land had dropped to £3.10s per annum, and the total Town Money available for distribution was £18.14s.2d. A revised list of fifty-four deserving parishioners was drawn up, giving them about 7s. each. By 1935, the distribution had fallen to 5s. per person. In 1942, it was decided that, in view of an increase in agricultural wages, the Town Money should be distributed to "old age pensioners, widows,

The High Street, 1914. The "Palace" on the left.

sick persons, and families with not less than two children or wives whose husbands were serving in the forces."

Lord Orford's and Tetsal's charities, hitherto charges on the Park estate, were redeemed in 1949 and the capital invested. In order to attract a tenant, the rental of the Poor's Land had remained absurdly low for many years. In 1958, Henry Simpson, the tenant, offered to pay 30s. per acre rent — a substantial increase. All the charities were registered with the Charity Commissioners in 1962.

Lord Orford's and Tetsal's charities now yield about £65 a year, and the Mercer's Company still pays the Revett bequest, now about £9 a year. Some years ago, the Gas Council paid for a wayleave across the Poor's Land which was invested to produced an annual income, and the Poor's Land is let at a realistic current agricultural rent. This enables about fifty villagers to receive, from the Town Money, a Christmas bonus of about £10.

J.S. Tharp's Charity — In 1873, Joseph Tharp gave £500 towards supplying coal to the deserving poor of Chippenham and Snailwell. This is the only charity covering both villages, and has therefore been managed separately from the Chippenham charities. The Charity Commissioners formulated a scheme in 1932, and the charity is administered by trustees from both villages.

Appendix 2
Listed buildings

Grade I

St. Margaret's church. C 12 and later.

Grade II*

The School House. late C 17.

Grade II

Chippenham Park:-
    The Hall — c. 1886-95.
    Landscaped park and gardens.
    Stable block — late C 17, converted to houses and flats.
    Dovecote — C 18.
    N.W. entrance gates and lodges — c. 1794-8.
    S. gateway and lodges — c. 1745. Sculpture — c. 1800.
High Street:-
    1-16, "New Row" — late C 18 or early C 19.
    17 — mid to late C 18.
    18-21 — "Maltings Yard" terrace contemporary with New Row recently rebuilt as a single house.
    22 — late C 16 farmhouse with later additions. The oldest house in the village, for many years the bakery.
    27 — "The Palace", early to mid C 18 with modern extension to N.W. So-called because it was at one time used by the bishop of Ely as a lodging when visiting the parish.
    36 — early C 17 farmhouse.
    37 — mid C 19 farmhouse.
    46 — Tharp Arms — early C 19.
    47 — early C 17, extended to north early C 19
    50 — early C 18.
Churchyard. Coping to C 13 tomb, E of S porch, believed to be tomb of one of the Knights Hospitallers.
        Seven tombstones in line S.W. of tower — early C 18. (There are many other decorative tombstones of the same era.)
        War memorial — c. 1920.

51 — Church Farmhouse — early to mid C 18, or possibly earlier.

52 — Enoch's Cottage — farmhouse dated 1673 on gable wall (now covered). Formerly known as Box Hall, renamed after the estate foreman c. 1920 (a popular clue for treasure hunters is "Mr. Powell doesn't live here")

52a — originally the bakehouse to the farmhouse.

New Street:-

7 — also 41 and 45 much altered — late C 17 or early C 18, possibly built by Lord Orford.

Snailwell road:-

Park Farmhouse — early C 19.

Phantom cottages — late C 18 or early C 19, of similar design to New Row.

Waterhall Farmhouse — late C 18 and mid C 20.

Badlingham Manor — late C 16 farmhouse with C 19 additions, surrounded by a moat.

Badlingham, thatched cottage — early C 17.

Chippenham Fen is now a National Nature Reserve with restricted access, though there is a public footpath across it.

The Russells, Baronets of Chippenham

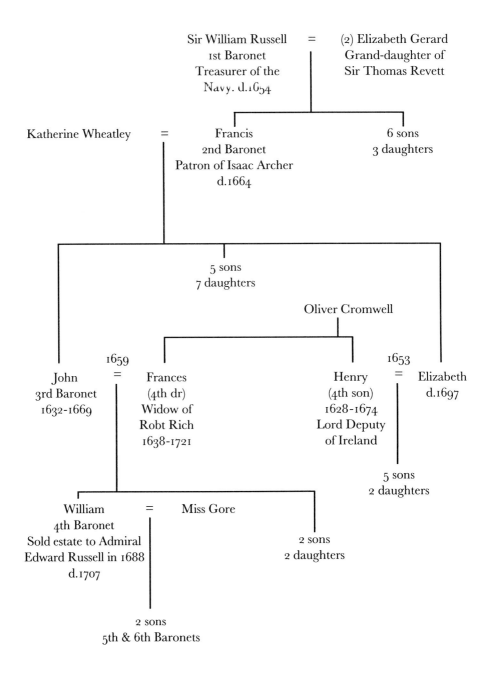

Sir William Russell   =   (2) Elizabeth Gerard
1st Baronet   Grand-daughter of
Treasurer of the   Sir Thomas Revett
Navy. d.1654

Katherine Wheatley   =   Francis   6 sons
2nd Baronet   3 daughters
Patron of Isaac Archer
d.1664

5 sons
7 daughters

Oliver Cromwell

John   1659   Frances   Henry   1653   Elizabeth
3rd Baronet   =   (4th dr)   (4th son)   =   d.1697
1632-1669   Widow of   1628-1674
Robt Rich   Lord Deputy
1638-1721   of Ireland

5 sons
2 daughters

William   =   Miss Gore
4th Baronet
Sold estate to Admiral   2 sons
Edward Russell in 1688   2 daughters
d.1707

2 sons
5th & 6th Baronets

The Tharps of Chippenham Park, Senior Branch

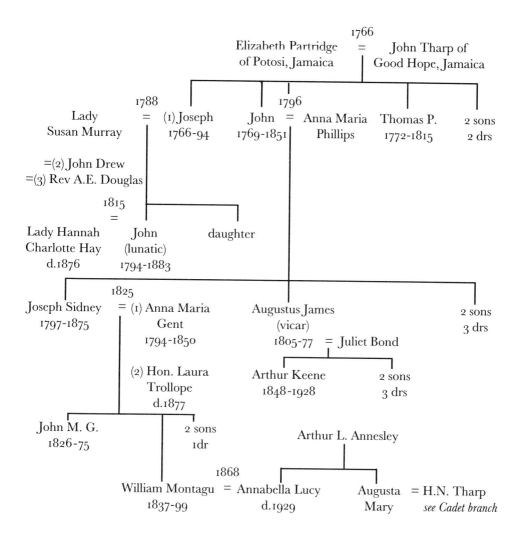

The Tharps of Chippeham Park, Cadet Branch

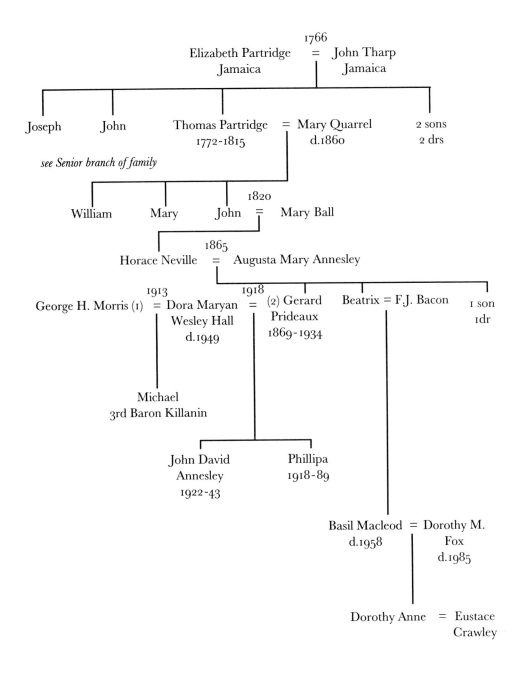